When Your Parent Has a Personality Disorder

Recovery Strategies for Adult Children of Narcissistic, Borderline, Antisocial, Paranoid, and All 10 Personality Disorders

Charlize Kaname McLean

Copyright © 2025 Charlize Kaname McLean. All rights reserved.
.

This book is for educational and informational purposes only and is not intended as medical, psychological, or therapeutic advice. The content is not meant to diagnose, treat, cure, or prevent any medical or psychological condition. Always consult with qualified mental health professionals regarding your specific situation. The author is not a licensed therapist, counselor, or medical professional.

 All case studies, examples, and personal stories presented in this book are composites created for illustrative purposes. Any resemblance to actual persons, living or deceased, is purely coincidental. Names including but not limited to Sarah, Michael, Lisa, David, Jennifer, Marcus, Amanda, Maya, Jonathan, Lauren, Robert, Emma, Rachel, Maria, Alex, Jordan, and all other individuals mentioned are fictional. While the therapeutic concepts and recovery approaches are based on established psychological principles, specific scenarios have been created to protect privacy and illustrate concepts.

The publisher and author make no representations or warranties of any kind with respect to this book or its contents. The publisher and author disclaim all liability in connection with the use of this book.

This work references numerous academic, clinical, and therapeutic sources. While every effort has been made to ensure accuracy, readers should verify information and consult current research and professional guidance for their individual circumstances.

ISBN: 978-1-7642471-1-5

Isohan Publishing

Table of Contents

Chapter 1: The Hidden Epidemic 1
    The Numbers Tell a Startling Story 1
    Why This Gap Exists 2
    Case Examples: Three Forgotten Stories 2
    The Unique Healing Challenge 4
    How to Use This Resource Safely 4
    Exercise: Initial Self-Assessment Checklist 5
    The Path Forward 7
    Bridge to Understanding 7

Chapter 2: When Love Hurts - Understanding Personality Disorders 9
    What Exactly Is a Personality Disorder 9
    The Three Clusters: Different Flavors of Dysfunction 10
    How Personality Disorders Sabotage Parenting 11
    Case Examples: When Love Gets Complicated 12
    Distinguishing Difficult from Disordered 14
    Common Myths That Keep You Stuck 15
    Exercise: Family Pattern Identification Worksheet 15
    The Healing Begins with Clarity 17
    Building Toward Healing 17

Chapter 3: The Lasting Impact - How We Carry Our Childhood ... 19
    The Science of Lasting Impact 19
    Common Adult Symptoms: The Childhood Connection 21
    Complex PTSD: When Trauma Is Relational 22

- Case Examples: How the Past Lives in the Present 23
- The Adaptation Trap...25
- Exercise: Personal Impact Inventory 26
- The Neurobiology of Hope..27
- Preparing for the Deep Work 28

Chapter 4: The Dramatic Cluster - When Emotions Rule 30
- Understanding Cluster B: The Emotional Tornado.....................30
- Borderline PD: Living on an Emotional Rollercoaster 31
- Histrionic PD: Life as Performance Art 33
- Narcissistic PD: Love With Conditions 34
- Antisocial PD: When Empathy Is Missing...................................36
- The Common Thread: Emotional Survival Training...................37
- Exercises: Pattern Identification and Emotional Flashback Log.38
- The Path Through Drama 40
- Transitioning to Calm 41

Chapter 5: The Anxious Cluster - When Fear Controls 42
- Understanding Cluster C: When Safety Becomes Prison...........42
- Avoidant PD: The Art of Emotional Distance 43
- Dependent PD: The Enmeshment Trap..44
- Obsessive-Compulsive PD: The Perfectionism Prison 46
- The Common Thread: Fear-Based Control 48
- The Perfectionism Spectrum 48
- Exercise: Boundary Assessment...49
- Exercise: Perfectionism Scale 50
- Breaking Free from Fear-Based Living......................................51
- The Gifts Hidden in Anxiety 52
- Case Study: Integration and Growth 52

Preparing for Complexity 53

Chapter 6: The Eccentric Cluster - When Reality Shifts 55

Understanding Cluster A: When Normal Becomes Strange 55

Paranoid PD: Living Under Siege 56

Schizoid PD: The Art of Emotional Invisibility 57

Schizotypal PD: When Thinking Gets Weird 59

The Common Thread: Reality Distortion 61

Exercise: Reality Testing Worksheet 61

Exercise: Social Skills Inventory 62

The Unique Challenge of Cluster A Recovery 64

The Hidden Gifts of Eccentric Families 64

Integration and Growth 65

Preparing for Complexity 66

Chapter 7: Mixed Messages - When Multiple Disorders Collide ... 68

When Disorders Multiply 68

Case Example: The Borderline-Narcissistic Parent 69

Case Example: The Two-Disorder Household 70

Substance Abuse: The Complicating Factor 70

Navigating Contradictory Demands 72

Both Parents with Disorders 72

Exercise: Family Dynamics Mapping 73

The Adaptation Advantages 74

The Identity Challenge 75

Healing the Fragmented Self 76

The Path to Integration 76

Preparing for the Developmental View 77

Chapter 8: Through a Child's Eyes - Developmental Impact 79

The Developing Brain Under Stress 79
Infancy (0-18 months): The Foundation of Trust 80
Early Childhood (18 months - 5 years): Identity Formation 81
School Age (6-11 years): Competence and Social Learning 83
Adolescence (12-18 years): Identity Integration and Independence 84
Young Adulthood (18-25 years): Launching and Intimacy 85
Exercise: Timeline of Impact Activity 86
The Neurobiological Legacy 88
Healing Across Developmental Stages 89
Integration and Hope 89
Moving into Healing 90

Chapter 9: Breaking the Spell - Recognizing Trauma Patterns 92

The Hidden Epidemic of Survival Responses 92
Common Coping Mechanisms and Their Hidden Costs 93
The Fawn Response Revolution 96
Exercise: Coping Inventory 97
Exercise: Trigger Identification 99
The Perfectionism Paradox 100
Depression and Anxiety as Trauma Responses 101
Breaking Free from Automatic Patterns 102
Bridging to Healing 102
Building Toward Solutions 103

Chapter 10: Therapeutic Approaches That Work 105

Why Standard Therapy Often Misses the Mark 105
Evidence-Based Approaches That Address PD Family Trauma 106

Dialectical Behavior Therapy Skills Training 106
Eye Movement Desensitization and Reprocessing 108
Internal Family Systems Therapy 110
Schema Therapy for Deep Pattern Change 111
Matching Therapy to Your PD Background 111
Finding Qualified Therapists 112
The Role of Medication 113
Exercise: Therapy Readiness Assessment 114
Integration and Hope 115
Preparing for Deep Work 116
Essential Learning Points 116

Chapter 11: The Reparenting Revolution 118
Understanding Self-Reparenting 118
What You Missed and Why It Matters 119
Case Example: Rebecca's Reparenting Journey 120
Meeting Unmet Developmental Needs 121
Case Example: David's Identity Recovery 122
Cultivating Self-Compassion 123
Building Internal Resources 125
Exercise: Inner Child Dialogue 126
Exercise: Self-Care Planning 127
The Transformation Process 129
Preparing for Boundaries 129
The Journey Continues 130
Core Transformations 130

Chapter 12: Boundaries - The Foundation of Recovery 132
Why Boundaries Feel Impossible 132

The Boundary Myths That Keep You Trapped 133
  Internal vs. External Boundaries 134
  PD-Specific Boundary Challenges 135
  Case Example: Tom's Narcissistic Father Boundaries 137
  Managing Guilt and Resistance 137
  Case Example: Linda's Dependent Mother Boundaries 138
  Boundary Scripts for Common Situations 139
  Exercise: Boundary Assessment 140
  Exercise: Boundary Practice Scenarios 141
  The Paradox of Healthy Boundaries 142
  Building Your Boundary Foundation 143

Chapter 13: Emotional Regulation Toolkit 145
  Understanding Your Inherited Nervous System 145
  The Three-Brain Model of Trauma Response 146
  DBT Skills by PD Background Type 147
  Case Example: Marcus's Emotional Regulation Journey 148
  Mindfulness and Grounding Techniques 149
  Flashback Management 150
  Distress Tolerance Building 152
  Case Example: Lisa's Distress Tolerance Development 153
  Exercise: TIPP Practice 154
  Exercise: Emotion Diary 155
  Building Your Regulation Toolkit 156
  Preparing for Relationship Healing 157
  Regulation Mastery Points 157

Chapter 14: Relationship Recovery 158
  Understanding Inherited Relationship Dynamics 158

Breaking Generational Patterns ... 159
Case Example: Breaking the Chaos Cycle ... 160
Identifying Inherited Dynamics ... 161
Case Example: Transforming the Control Cycle ... 162
Building Secure Attachments ... 162
Case Example: Developing Secure Attachment ... 164
Conscious Parenting Approaches ... 164
Exercise: Pattern Analysis ... 166
Exercise: Communication Practice ... 167
The Paradox of Relationship Recovery ... 168
Preparing for Daily Practices ... 168
Relationship Recovery Foundations ... 169

Chapter 15: Daily Practices for Long-term Healing ... 170
The Science of Sustainable Change ... 170
Creating Your Healing Routine Foundation ... 171
Case Example: Robert's Routine Development ... 172
Support Group Navigation ... 173
Case Example: Maria's Support Group Journey ... 175
Self-Advocacy Skills Development ... 175
Case Example: Jennifer's Self-Advocacy Development ... 176
Community Building ... 177
Exercise: Daily Check-in System ... 178
Exercise: Support Mapping ... 179
Sustaining Your Practice ... 181
Preparing for Integration ... 182
Daily Practice Foundations ... 182

Chapter 16: Post-Traumatic Growth - Thriving Beyond Survival 184

Understanding Post-Traumatic Growth 184
From Victim to Thriver Journey 185
Case Example: Marcus's Transformation Journey 187
Meaning-Making from Trauma 188
Case Example: Sarah's Meaning-Making Process 188
Helping Others Heal 189
Case Example: Jennifer's Balanced Approach to Helping 190
Setback Navigation 191
Life Vision Creation 192
Exercise: Values Clarification 193
Exercise: Future Visualization 194
The Paradox of Gratitude 195
The Ongoing Journey 195
Reflection and Integration 195

Referencee 198

Chapter 1: The Hidden Epidemic

Sarah stared at her phone screen, her thumb hovering over the "add to cart" button for yet another book about narcissistic parents. She'd already read seventeen of them. Each one helped a little, but something felt incomplete—like trying to solve a puzzle with missing pieces. Her mother wasn't just demanding attention or lacking empathy. She was obsessed with perfection, controlling every detail of Sarah's life with rigid rules and impossible standards. The narcissism books touched on control, but they didn't capture the suffocating perfectionism that defined her childhood. Sarah needed answers for what felt like a different kind of prison entirely.

What Sarah didn't know is that she represents millions of adults searching for healing resources that simply don't exist. While bookstore shelves overflow with guides for survivors of narcissistic parents, those raised by parents with other personality disorders face a stark reality—their specific experiences remain largely invisible.

The Numbers Tell a Startling Story

Research from the American Academy of Family Physicians and Psychiatric News reveals that personality disorders affect approximately 10-15% of the adult population. This translates to millions of parents whose disorders profoundly shape their children's development. Yet the publishing industry has fixated almost exclusively on narcissistic personality disorder (NPD) and borderline personality disorder (BPD), leaving enormous gaps in available resources.

Consider these overlooked populations:

- **16.4 million adults** raised by parents with Obsessive-Compulsive Personality Disorder (OCPD)—the perfectionistic controllers who made love conditional on achievement
- **7.6 million adults** who survived antisocial parents—those who lacked empathy and manipulated without conscience

- **4.9 million adults** raised by avoidant parents—the emotionally distant figures who taught isolation as survival
- **3.2 million adults** who experienced dependent parents—those who reversed roles and made their children the caretakers

The math is sobering. When we account for all ten personality disorders, we're looking at 28.2 million adult children in need of specialized healing resources. The current market serves perhaps 15% of this population, leaving 85% searching for answers that address their specific childhood experiences.

Why This Gap Exists

The publishing world operates on market signals, and narcissistic abuse has captured public attention in ways other personality disorders haven't. NPD gets coverage because the behaviors are dramatic and easily recognized. The grandiose narcissist makes for compelling reading. The manipulative borderline parent creates page-turning drama. But what about the quietly perfectionistic OCPD parent whose love came with impossible standards? The antisocial parent who taught manipulation as normal family interaction? These stories lack the theatrical elements that drive bestseller lists, yet they cause equally profound damage.

This oversight isn't just unfortunate—it's harmful. Adult children of personality-disordered parents develop symptoms and coping mechanisms specific to their particular childhood environment. The hypervigilance learned from a paranoid parent differs markedly from the perfectionism inherited from an OCPD parent. Generic trauma healing approaches miss these nuances entirely.

Case Examples: Three Forgotten Stories

Michael's OCPD Mother

Michael, now 34, grew up with a mother whose obsession with order and perfection controlled every aspect of family life. Breakfast had to be eaten by 7:15 AM exactly. Homework required three drafts minimum. His bedroom faced daily inspection, with points deducted for dust on baseboards or books not aligned perfectly on shelves. Love came with performance reviews—literally. His mother kept charts tracking his grades, chores, and behavior, with affection dispensed based on scores.

Today, Michael struggles with decision paralysis. He spends hours crafting emails, rewriting them multiple times before hitting send. He's changed careers four times, always convinced he's not meeting some invisible standard. Traditional therapy helped with general anxiety, but nothing addressed the specific prison of perfectionism that shaped his worldview. Books about narcissistic parents discussed control, but missed the particular torture of never being "good enough" no matter how hard he tried.

Lisa's Antisocial Father

Lisa learned early that survival meant reading people quickly and accurately. Her father viewed every interaction as a transaction to be won. He taught her to lie convincingly by age eight, to charm adults into giving her what she wanted, and to manipulate situations to her advantage. He wasn't absent or neglectful—quite the opposite. He was intensely involved in teaching her his worldview that people were either useful or obstacles.

Now 29, Lisa struggles with authentic relationships. She automatically assesses what people want from her and adjusts her personality accordingly. She's successful professionally—her father's lessons in reading and influencing people translated well to sales—but she feels like a fraud in personal relationships. She knows how to make people like her, but doesn't know how to simply be herself. Resources for children of narcissistic parents focus on recovering self-worth, but Lisa's challenge runs deeper—she needs to discover an authentic self beneath layers of learned manipulation.

David's Avoidant Parents

David's household was quiet. Not peaceful quiet—hollow quiet. His parents interacted with him only when necessary, maintaining physical care while offering no emotional connection. They didn't fight, didn't express affection, didn't share feelings or interests. Family dinners happened in silence. Conversations focused purely on logistics: schedules, schoolwork, necessities. When David tried to share excitement about achievements or concerns about problems, his parents listened politely and offered brief, practical responses before changing the subject.

At 31, David finds social connections exhausting and confusing. He intellectually understands that people form emotional bonds, but the mechanics feel foreign. He's developed successful coping strategies—he's reliable, competent, and kind—but relationships feel like acting. He can perform the motions of friendship and romantic connection, but the emotional reciprocity that others seem to experience naturally requires enormous effort. Books about healing from narcissistic or borderline parents assume a foundation of emotional awareness that David never developed.

The Unique Healing Challenge

Each personality disorder creates distinct developmental disruptions that require specific healing approaches. The adult child of an OCPD parent needs to unlearn perfectionism and develop self-compassion around "good enough." The adult child of an antisocial parent needs to rebuild their ability to trust their own moral compass and form authentic connections. The adult child of avoidant parents needs to develop emotional vocabulary and connection skills from scratch.

Generic trauma healing approaches can help with symptoms—anxiety, depression, relationship difficulties—but they miss the underlying patterns that created these symptoms. It's like treating a broken bone without understanding how it was broken. You might reduce pain and restore some function, but without addressing the specific injury mechanism, healing remains incomplete.

How to Use This Resource Safely

This book covers difficult territory. Reading about parental personality disorders can trigger intense emotional responses, including:

- Grief over recognizing the childhood you deserved but didn't receive
- Anger toward your parent that feels overwhelming or scary
- Guilt about "pathologizing" someone you love
- Fear that you've inherited the same disorders
- Shame about your family's dysfunction becoming visible

Safety Guidelines:

1. **Read at your own pace**. This information will be here when you're ready for it.
2. **Have support available**. Consider working with a therapist familiar with personality disorders and childhood trauma.
3. **Practice grounding techniques**. If you feel overwhelmed, try the 5-4-3-2-1 technique: name 5 things you can see, 4 things you can touch, 3 things you can hear, 2 things you can smell, and 1 thing you can taste.
4. **Avoid self-diagnosis**. This book helps you understand your experiences, not diagnose your parent.
5. **Focus on your healing**. You can't change your parent, but you can change how their disorder continues to affect your life.

Exercise: Initial Self-Assessment Checklist

This assessment helps identify which chapters might be most relevant to your experience. Check the statements that resonate with your childhood:

Perfectionist/Controlling Environment:

- [ ] Love felt conditional on performance or achievement
- [ ] Small mistakes led to disproportionate reactions
- [ ] Rules were rigid and numerous
- [ ] "Good enough" was never actually good enough

- [ ] You felt like you were walking on eggshells around standards

Manipulative/Exploitative Environment:

- [ ] You learned to lie or manipulate to avoid conflict
- [ ] Your parent seemed to lack empathy for others' pain
- [ ] You were taught that people are either useful or obstacles
- [ ] Your parent had frequent legal or financial troubles
- [ ] You felt like a tool for your parent's goals rather than a person

Emotionally Distant Environment:

- [ ] Your parent was physically present but emotionally absent
- [ ] Expressing emotions was discouraged or ignored
- [ ] Family interactions focused on logistics, not connection
- [ ] You learned early that your feelings didn't matter
- [ ] Affection felt awkward or performative

Dramatic/Chaotic Environment:

- [ ] Your parent's emotions dominated family life
- [ ] You became the parent in the relationship
- [ ] Crises happened frequently and intensely
- [ ] Your parent competed with you for attention
- [ ] Family life felt like a soap opera you couldn't escape

Suspicious/Paranoid Environment:

- [ ] Your parent saw threats and conspiracies everywhere
- [ ] You were taught to distrust others' motives
- [ ] Your parent isolated the family from outside influences
- [ ] Questions about your parent's suspicions were discouraged
- [ ] You learned hypervigilance as a survival skill

Your responses point toward the chapters most relevant to your healing journey. But don't skip the others—personality disorders often overlap, and understanding the full spectrum helps you recognize patterns you might have normalized.

The Path Forward

Sarah eventually found this book. She discovered that her mother's perfectionistic control wasn't a form of narcissism—it was OCPD. The distinction mattered enormously. NPD recovery focuses on rebuilding self-worth after being devalued. OCPD recovery focuses on permission to be imperfect after being held to impossible standards. Similar symptoms, different healing paths.

You deserve resources that address your specific experience. You deserve to understand how your particular childhood shaped you and what specific skills you need to heal. Most importantly, you deserve to know that your experience is real, your pain is valid, and your healing is possible.

The epidemic isn't just personality disorders in parents—it's the silence around most of them. By reading this book, you're ending that silence in your own life. You're choosing to understand your story fully so you can rewrite your future authentically.

Bridge to Understanding

Now that you understand the scope of this hidden epidemic, you're ready to learn exactly what personality disorders are and how they affect parenting. Not every difficult parent has a personality disorder, and not every personality disorder creates the same parenting challenges. The next chapter will help you distinguish between normal human struggles and the persistent patterns that define personality disorders—patterns that shaped your childhood in specific and predictable ways.

Key Insights

- **28.2 million adults** need healing resources for non-narcissistic personality-disordered parents, but 85% of available resources focus on NPD/BPD only
- Each personality disorder creates **distinct developmental disruptions** requiring specific healing approaches
- Generic trauma healing misses the **underlying patterns** that created symptoms
- Your healing path depends on understanding **your specific childhood environment**, not just general family dysfunction
- Reading about personality disorders can trigger intense emotions—**proceed at your own pace** with support available

Chapter 2: When Love Hurts - Understanding Personality Disorders

The phone call came at 2 AM, which wasn't unusual. What surprised Rachel was the calm desperation in her sister's voice. "I need you to explain something to me," Maya said. "I've been reading about personality disorders, and I think I understand why Mom acted the way she did. But I don't understand how someone can love you and hurt you at the same time."

This question captures the heart of what makes growing up with a personality-disordered parent so confusing. Your parent likely loved you. They probably tried their best according to their understanding of love and family. Yet their "love" came wrapped in patterns that caused lasting harm. The confusion isn't your fault—it's the natural result of receiving care that simultaneously nourishes and wounds.

What Exactly Is a Personality Disorder

Personality disorders represent deeply ingrained patterns of thinking, feeling, and behaving that differ markedly from cultural expectations and cause significant distress or impairment. Think of personality as your default operating system—the automatic ways you interpret situations, respond to stress, and relate to others. Most people's operating systems are flexible enough to adapt to different circumstances while maintaining core stability.

Personality disorders represent operating systems that became fixed in childhood and resist updating. The person experiences their patterns as normal and natural—"This is just who I am"—even when these patterns consistently create problems in relationships, work, and daily life.

Three key features define personality disorders:

1. **Pervasiveness**: The patterns show up across multiple areas of life, not just in specific situations

2. **Persistence**: The patterns remain stable over time, typically beginning by early adulthood
3. **Problematic**: The patterns cause significant distress to the person or those around them

The Three Clusters: Different Flavors of Dysfunction

Mental health professionals organize personality disorders into three clusters based on similar characteristics:

Cluster A: The Odd and Eccentric These disorders involve unusual thinking and behavior that others find strange or difficult to understand:

- **Paranoid PD**: Pervasive distrust and suspicion of others
- **Schizoid PD**: Detachment from social relationships and restricted emotional expression
- **Schizotypal PD**: Acute discomfort with close relationships, cognitive distortions, and eccentric behavior

Cluster B: The Dramatic and Erratic
These disorders involve emotional instability, dramatic behavior, and troubled relationships:

- **Borderline PD**: Instability in relationships, self-image, and emotions with marked impulsivity
- **Narcissistic PD**: Grandiose sense of self-importance, need for admiration, lack of empathy
- **Histrionic PD**: Excessive emotional expression and attention-seeking behavior
- **Antisocial PD**: Disregard for and violation of others' rights

Cluster C: The Anxious and Fearful These disorders involve anxiety, fear, and rigid behavior patterns:

- **Avoidant PD**: Social inhibition, feelings of inadequacy, hypersensitivity to criticism

- **Dependent PD**: Excessive need to be taken care of leading to submissive behavior
- **Obsessive-Compulsive PD**: Preoccupation with orderliness, perfectionism, and control

How Personality Disorders Sabotage Parenting

Healthy parenting requires flexibility, emotional regulation, empathy, and the ability to prioritize a child's needs over one's own immediate wants. Personality disorders interfere with each of these capacities in predictable ways.

Flexibility Becomes Rigidity Children need parents who can adapt their approach based on the child's developmental stage, temperament, and current needs. A toddler requires different responses than a teenager. A sensitive child needs different handling than an extroverted one. Personality disorders create rigid response patterns that can't adjust to changing circumstances.

Emotional Dysregulation Creates Chaos Children learn emotional regulation by watching their parents model it. They need to see how healthy adults handle frustration, disappointment, anger, and sadness. When a parent's emotions are consistently explosive, unpredictable, or shut down entirely, children learn maladaptive emotional patterns or become hypervigilant to emotional cues.

Empathy Deficits Block Attunement Healthy parents can sense what their child is experiencing emotionally and respond appropriately. This attunement helps children develop secure attachment and emotional intelligence. Personality disorders often impair this empathic capacity, leaving children feeling unseen and misunderstood.

Self-Focus Overrides Child Focus Effective parenting requires putting the child's needs first, at least much of the time. Parents with personality disorders often unconsciously make the child responsible for meeting the parent's emotional needs—for attention, validation, caretaking, or emotional regulation.

Case Examples: When Love Gets Complicated

Jennifer's Histrionic Mother

Jennifer's mother loved being a mom—or rather, she loved the attention that came with being a dramatic, devoted mother. School events became performances where Mom was the star. When Jennifer got sick, Mom transformed into Florence Nightingale, complete with elaborate care routines and social media documentation. When Jennifer achieved something, Mom's excitement was so over-the-top that Jennifer learned to downplay her accomplishments to avoid the theatrical response.

The love was real. Mom genuinely delighted in Jennifer and wanted to care for her. But the love came filtered through Mom's need for attention and drama. Jennifer learned that her experiences only mattered if they could serve her mother's emotional needs. Good news had to be celebration-worthy. Bad news had to be tragedy-worthy. Ordinary childhood experiences—the quiet satisfactions, small disappointments, and daily growth—got ignored because they didn't provide sufficient emotional fuel.

Now 28, Jennifer struggles with a persistent sense that her life isn't "enough." She finds herself manufacturing drama to feel interesting, then feeling exhausted by the intensity she's created. She intellectually knows that peaceful, ordinary moments have value, but emotionally she feels like she's disappearing if life gets too calm.

Marcus's OCPD Father

Marcus's father showed love through high standards and meticulous attention to detail. He spent hours helping with homework, ensuring every assignment met his exacting requirements. He researched the best equipment for Marcus's sports teams, the most effective study methods, the optimal nutrition plans. He truly wanted Marcus to excel and was willing to invest enormous time and energy in that goal.

But his love came with conditions that were impossible to meet. "Good" wasn't good enough—only "perfect" qualified as acceptable. B+ grades led to detailed analysis of what went wrong. Second place finishes resulted in training plan modifications. Even successes got dissected to identify areas for improvement. Marcus learned that love was something you earned through performance, and that earning it today didn't guarantee having it tomorrow.

Marcus, now 35, experiences anxiety around any situation that might be evaluated—job interviews, performance reviews, even casual games with friends. He's professionally successful because he learned to work harder than anyone else, but he can't enjoy his achievements. Each success simply raises the bar for what's required next time. He intellectually knows his father loved him, but that love felt more like a contract with impossible terms than an unconditional gift.

Amanda's Avoidant Mother

Amanda's mother provided excellent physical care. Meals appeared on schedule, clothes were clean and appropriate, medical needs were met promptly. Mom was consistently present, rarely raising her voice or creating drama. From the outside, it looked like attentive, stable parenting.

But emotional connection was absent. Mom responded to Amanda's excitement about school achievements with brief acknowledgment before changing the subject. When Amanda faced social problems or developmental challenges, Mom offered practical solutions without emotional support. Conversations focused on logistics and schedules. Physical affection was minimal and felt awkward when it occurred.

Amanda learned that emotions were private matters that shouldn't be shared. She developed self-reliance as a survival skill, becoming the child who never caused problems or asked for much. She interpreted her mother's emotional distance as evidence that she was fundamentally unworthy of deeper connection.

At 32, Amanda maintains successful but superficial relationships. She's the friend others call for practical help or reliable company, but intimate emotional sharing feels foreign and uncomfortable. She can provide support to others but struggles to receive it. She knows her mother loved her in her limited way, but that love felt more like benevolent caregiving than genuine emotional connection.

Distinguishing Difficult from Disordered

Not every challenging parent has a personality disorder. All parents have difficult moments, personal struggles, and areas where they fall short of ideal parenting. The distinction lies in patterns, persistence, and pervasiveness.

Difficult but Not Disordered:

- Problems appear in specific areas or during stressful periods
- The parent can recognize when their behavior is problematic
- The parent makes genuine efforts to change when issues are pointed out
- The parent's identity isn't built around the problematic patterns
- Good periods provide genuine relief and connection

Potentially Disordered:

- Problems appear consistently across time and situations
- The parent sees their patterns as normal and justified
- Attempts to address problems are met with defensiveness or blame-shifting
- The parent's identity is organized around these patterns
- "Good" periods often serve the parent's needs rather than genuinely connecting with the child

Consider the difference between a parent who struggles with perfectionism during stressful periods (difficult) versus a parent whose entire identity revolves around maintaining impossible standards (potentially OCPD). Or a parent who occasionally seeks too much attention (difficult) versus a parent who consistently makes themselves the center of every situation (potentially histrionic).

Common Myths That Keep You Stuck

Myth 1: "They meant well, so the impact doesn't matter" Good intentions don't erase harmful impact. Your parent likely did mean well according to their limited understanding. But meaning well while consistently causing harm points to something deeper than occasional parenting mistakes.

Myth 2: "It wasn't that bad compared to other people's childhoods" Comparison minimizes your experience and blocks healing. The question isn't whether others had it worse—it's whether your childhood gave you what you needed to develop into a healthy adult.

Myth 3: "I should be grateful they provided for me" Meeting basic physical needs is the minimum requirement for parenting, not something that earns gratitude or excuses emotional harm. You can acknowledge that your parent did some things well while also recognizing the areas where they failed you.

Myth 4: "If I understand their childhood trauma, I should forgive them" Understanding why someone acts harmfully doesn't obligate you to excuse the harm or maintain relationship patterns that continue to hurt you. Compassion for their struggles and protection of your own wellbeing can coexist.

Myth 5: "They couldn't help it because of their disorder" Personality disorders make certain behaviors more likely, but they don't remove all choice or responsibility. Many people with personality disorders recognize their patterns and work to minimize harm to others, especially their children.

Exercise: Family Pattern Identification Worksheet

This exercise helps you identify consistent patterns in your family environment rather than isolated incidents. For each category, note specific examples and how frequently they occurred:

Emotional Patterns:

- How did your parent typically respond to your emotions (excitement, sadness, anger, fear)?
- What emotions were acceptable to express? Which were discouraged or punished?
- How did your parent manage their own emotions around you?

Relationship Patterns:

- How did your parent relate to other adults (spouse, friends, family, authorities)?
- What did you learn about trust, boundaries, and intimacy from watching them?
- How did they handle conflict or disagreement?

Communication Patterns:

- What topics were safe to discuss? Which were off-limits?
- How much emotional sharing happened in your family?
- Did conversations focus more on logistics or on feelings and experiences?

Love and Approval Patterns:

- What earned your parent's approval or affection?
- Did love feel conditional on your behavior, achievement, or compliance?
- How did your parent show care or concern for your wellbeing?

Control and Autonomy Patterns:

- How much input did you have in decisions that affected you?
- Were your preferences, opinions, and choices respected?

- How did your parent respond when you asserted independence?

Look for themes that persisted across years and situations. These patterns, more than individual incidents, shaped your development and continue to influence your adult life.

The Healing Begins with Clarity

Rachel's sister Maya needed to understand that love and harm can coexist because personality disorders create exactly this confusion. The parent genuinely loves the child but expresses that love through a distorted lens that consistently misses the mark. The love is real, but it's filtered through patterns that prioritize the parent's needs over the child's developmental requirements.

This understanding doesn't diminish your parent's love or your relationship with them. Instead, it provides clarity about why their love felt complicated and why you might struggle with specific areas of adult functioning. You can hold love for your parent alongside recognition that their parenting caused harm. Both truths can exist simultaneously.

Understanding personality disorders also helps you recognize that your childhood struggles weren't your fault. You weren't too sensitive, too demanding, or too difficult. You were a child trying to adapt to a family system organized around patterns that couldn't consistently meet your developmental needs.

Building Toward Healing

Now that you understand what personality disorders are and how they affect parenting, you're ready to explore the lasting impact these early experiences have on adult functioning. The patterns you learned in childhood continue to influence how you think, feel, and relate to others today. But unlike personality disorders themselves, these learned patterns can change with understanding and intentional practice.

The next chapter examines how the adaptations you made to survive your childhood—the hypervigilance, people-pleasing, emotional numbing, or perfectionism—continue to operate in your adult life, often causing problems in situations where they're no longer necessary for survival.

Key Insights

- Personality disorders represent **fixed operating systems** that resist updating and cause consistent problems across relationships and situations
- Each cluster creates **specific parenting challenges**: odd/eccentric parents struggle with connection, dramatic/erratic parents create emotional chaos, anxious/fearful parents impose rigid restrictions
- **Love and harm can coexist**—parents with personality disorders often genuinely love their children but express it through distorted patterns that miss developmental needs
- The distinction between difficult and disordered lies in **patterns, persistence, and pervasiveness** rather than isolated incidents
- Understanding your parent's disorder **doesn't excuse the harm** but provides clarity about why their love felt complicated and why specific adult struggles persist

Chapter 3: The Lasting Impact - How We Carry Our Childhood

Dr. Elena Martinez thought she had successfully left her childhood behind. At 35, she was a respected pediatrician with a thriving practice, a loving marriage, and two healthy children. Her colleagues admired her diagnostic skills and gentle bedside manner. Parents trusted her completely. She appeared to have everything together.

But success couldn't quiet the voice in her head that analyzed every interaction for signs of disapproval. It couldn't stop the panic that flooded her system whenever her supervisor scheduled a meeting, even for routine matters. It couldn't explain why she worked until exhaustion to ensure every patient chart was perfect, or why she apologized constantly for things that weren't her fault.

Elena's childhood with a paranoid, controlling mother had ended twenty years ago, yet its influence showed up daily in her adult life. Like millions of others raised by personality-disordered parents, she discovered that leaving home doesn't automatically mean leaving the patterns behind.

The Science of Lasting Impact

Research consistently shows that parental personality disorders create specific and predictable impacts on child development that persist into adulthood. This isn't about blame or weakness—it's about understanding how the human brain adapts to survive challenging environments.

Attachment Theory Foundation

Attachment theory explains how early relationships with caregivers create internal working models that guide future relationships. Children develop expectations about whether others are trustworthy, whether they themselves are worthy of love, and whether relationships are safe or dangerous.

Secure attachment develops when caregivers are consistently responsive, emotionally available, and able to regulate their own emotions. The child learns: "I am worthy of love, others are generally trustworthy, and relationships are safe spaces where I can be authentic."

Personality disorders interfere with the consistent, attuned caregiving required for secure attachment. Instead, children develop insecure attachment patterns:

- **Anxious attachment**: "I need others desperately but can't count on them being there consistently"
- **Avoidant attachment**: "I can't depend on others, so I'll rely only on myself"
- **Disorganized attachment**: "Relationships are simultaneously necessary and terrifying"

These attachment patterns become templates for adult relationships, influencing everything from romantic partnerships to workplace dynamics.

Neurobiological Changes

Growing up in chronically stressful environments actually changes brain development. The child's nervous system adapts to prioritize survival over learning, growth, and connection.

Key changes include:

- **Hyperactive amygdala**: The brain's alarm system becomes oversensitive, triggering fight-or-flight responses to minor stressors
- **Underdeveloped prefrontal cortex**: The area responsible for emotional regulation and decision-making doesn't fully mature
- **Altered stress hormone patterns**: Cortisol and adrenaline systems become dysregulated
- **Changed neural pathways**: The brain becomes wired for hypervigilance rather than calm presence

These changes helped you survive childhood but can create problems in adult environments where hypervigilance isn't necessary and may actually interfere with functioning.

Common Adult Symptoms: The Childhood Connection

Adult children of personality-disordered parents often struggle with similar symptoms regardless of the specific disorder involved. These symptoms represent logical adaptations to illogical family systems.

Anxiety and Hypervigilance Growing up with unpredictable or threatening parents teaches children to constantly scan for danger. This hypervigilance continues into adulthood as chronic anxiety, difficulty relaxing, and an exhausting need to monitor others' moods and reactions.

You might find yourself:

- Analyzing conversations for hidden meanings
- Feeling responsible for others' emotional states
- Having difficulty being present because part of your attention is always scanning for threats
- Feeling anxious in situations that others find normal or enjoyable

Depression and Emotional Numbing Children who learn that their emotions don't matter or cause problems often develop sophisticated numbing strategies. This emotional suppression can continue into adulthood as depression, emptiness, or disconnection from feelings.

You might experience:

- Difficulty identifying what you're feeling beyond "good" or "bad"
- A sense that life lacks meaning or purpose
- Feeling like you're going through the motions without genuine engagement

- Periodic episodes of overwhelming sadness that seem to come from nowhere

Relationship Difficulties Growing up with disordered relationship patterns teaches children confusing and contradictory lessons about connection. These early lessons create predictable adult relationship challenges.

Common patterns include:

- Choosing partners who recreate familiar dynamics from childhood
- Difficulty with boundaries—either too rigid or too permeable
- People-pleasing to avoid conflict or abandonment
- Feeling responsible for others' emotions while neglecting your own needs
- Either avoiding intimacy entirely or becoming quickly enmeshed

Identity and Self-Worth Issues

Children develop their sense of self largely through their parents' eyes. Personality-disordered parents often can't see their children clearly, leading to identity confusion and self-worth problems.

You might struggle with:

- Not knowing who you really are beneath learned adaptations
- Feeling like a fraud or imposter in your achievements
- Difficulty making decisions because you don't trust your own judgment
- Persistent shame about being "defective" or "too much"

Complex PTSD: When Trauma Is Relational

Traditional PTSD results from specific traumatic events. Complex PTSD (C-PTSD) develops from ongoing relational trauma, particularly in childhood. Growing up with a personality-disordered parent often creates C-PTSD because the trauma comes from the relationship itself rather than specific incidents.

C-PTSD symptoms include:

1. **Emotional Dysregulation**: Difficulty managing emotions, extreme reactions to stress, emotional numbing
2. **Interpersonal Problems**: Difficulty trusting others, fear of abandonment, problems with boundaries
3. **Negative Self-Concept**: Persistent shame, self-blame, feeling fundamentally flawed
4. **Disrupted Attention and Consciousness**: Difficulty concentrating, dissociation, memory problems
5. **Behavioral Control Issues**: Self-destructive behaviors, difficulty with impulse control
6. **Meaning-Making Difficulties**: Loss of faith, hopelessness about the future, existential despair

Unlike single-incident trauma that can often be processed and integrated, relational trauma becomes part of your core operating system. It affects not just how you react to specific triggers, but how you fundamentally understand yourself and relationships.

Case Examples: How the Past Lives in the Present

Marcus and Work Performance

Marcus, whose OCPD father we met in Chapter 2, became a successful software engineer. His attention to detail and willingness to work long hours made him valuable to employers. But his perfectionism created constant misery.

Every code review felt like a judgment of his worth as a person. Minor bugs in his programs triggered shame spirals that lasted for days. He regularly stayed late to polish work that was already excellent, unable to submit anything that wasn't perfect. When colleagues made casual suggestions, Marcus heard criticism and launched into lengthy explanations of his choices.

His manager, Sarah, was puzzled by his reactions. Marcus was clearly talented, but he seemed to assume that she was constantly evaluating him negatively. Simple requests like "Can you look into this issue?" prompted anxiety-driven over-responses that concerned her. She wanted to promote Marcus but worried about his ability to handle the increased responsibility given his obvious stress around performance evaluation.

Marcus's childhood programming told him that love and approval came only through flawless performance. His nervous system couldn't distinguish between his father's impossible standards and his manager's reasonable expectations. Every workplace interaction activated childhood survival strategies that were no longer necessary but had become automatic.

Jennifer and Romantic Relationships

Jennifer, whose histrionic mother required dramatic presentations of love, struggled to believe that quiet affection was genuine. In relationships, she unconsciously escalated emotions to feel connected. Small disagreements became relationship-threatening crises. Good news required celebration worthy of major milestones. Ordinary Tuesday evenings felt like abandonment.

Her partner, David, loved Jennifer but felt exhausted by the emotional intensity she required. He couldn't understand why his consistent, reliable affection didn't feel reassuring to her. When he wanted quiet time together, Jennifer interpreted his calm presence as disinterest. When he responded to her excitement with gentle pleasure rather than matching her intensity, she felt unloved.

Jennifer had learned that love looked dramatic and feelings needed to be performed at high volume to be valid. Her nervous system interpreted David's steady, peaceful love as emotional absence because it didn't match the chaotic intensity she'd learned to associate with caring. She intellectually knew that David loved her, but emotionally she felt loved only during their intense conversations or dramatic reconciliations.

Amanda and Parenting Struggles

Amanda, raised by emotionally avoidant parents, desperately wanted to be different with her own children. She read parenting books, attended classes, and intellectually understood the importance of emotional connection. But when her five-year-old son had a meltdown, Amanda's instinct was to solve the problem rather than provide emotional comfort.

She could efficiently address logistics—finding lost toys, negotiating bedtime routines, managing schedules. But when her son needed emotional support for friendship drama or fears about starting school, Amanda felt lost. She wanted to provide comfort but didn't have a template for emotional soothing because she'd never received it.

Her son began taking his emotional needs to his father, who was more naturally attuned to feelings. Amanda felt hurt and inadequate, wondering why she couldn't access the maternal warmth that seemed to come naturally to other mothers. She loved her children intensely but struggled to express that love in ways they could receive.

Amanda's childhood had taught her that practical care was love and that emotions were private matters to be handled independently. Despite her conscious intentions, her nervous system defaulted to the patterns she'd learned, leaving her feeling incompetent in the area of parenting she most wanted to master.

The Adaptation Trap

The symptoms that create problems in adult life often represent brilliant adaptations to impossible childhood circumstances. Your hypervigilance protected you from your parent's unpredictable moods. Your people-pleasing prevented conflicts that felt dangerous. Your emotional numbing helped you survive situations that would have overwhelmed a developing nervous system.

These adaptations weren't mistakes—they were survival strategies that worked in their original context. The problem arises when you continue using childhood survival strategies in adult situations that don't require them. Your nervous system can't always distinguish between past danger and present safety, so it continues running programs designed for a threatening environment.

This creates the adaptation trap: the very strategies that helped you survive childhood now interfere with thriving in adulthood. Breaking free requires updating your nervous system's threat assessment and learning new strategies appropriate for your current life.

Exercise: Personal Impact Inventory

This exercise helps you identify how your childhood experiences continue to influence your adult life. For each area, note specific patterns without judgment—you're gathering information, not criticizing yourself.

Physical Symptoms:

- How does your body respond to stress? (tension, headaches, digestive issues, sleep problems)
- Do you have chronic health issues that might be stress-related?
- How well do you take care of your physical needs (nutrition, exercise, medical care)?

Emotional Patterns:

- Which emotions feel safe to experience and express?
- Which emotions trigger shame, fear, or numbness?
- How do you typically cope with difficult feelings?

Relationship Patterns:

- What attracts you to certain people?
- How do you behave when you feel threatened in relationships?
- What's your default response to conflict?

Work and Achievement:

- How do you respond to feedback or evaluation?
- What drives your work habits and career choices?
- How do you handle success and failure?

Self-Care and Boundaries:

- How well do you recognize and communicate your needs?
- What makes boundary-setting difficult?
- How do you treat yourself when you make mistakes?

Parenting (if applicable):

- Which aspects of parenting feel natural versus difficult?
- How do you respond when your children express strong emotions?
- What patterns from your childhood do you see yourself repeating or avoiding?

Look for themes that connect your current struggles to your childhood experiences. This isn't about self-blame—it's about understanding how the past continues to influence the present so you can make conscious choices about the future.

The Neurobiology of Hope

The same neuroplasticity that allowed your brain to adapt to challenging circumstances also makes healing possible. Adult brains retain the ability to form new neural pathways and update old patterns when given appropriate support and practice.

Healing doesn't require erasing your childhood or becoming a different person. Instead, it involves:

- **Understanding your patterns** so you can respond consciously rather than reactively
- **Updating your nervous system's threat assessment** to distinguish between past danger and present safety

- **Learning new skills** appropriate for your current life circumstances
- **Developing self-compassion** for the adaptations that helped you survive

Dr. Elena Martinez eventually learned that her hypervigilance, while exhausting, had also contributed to her diagnostic abilities and patient advocacy skills. Her healing journey wasn't about eliminating these traits but rather gaining conscious control over them. She could choose when to activate her heightened attention and when to relax into trust.

This is the promise of recovery: not becoming someone different, but becoming more fully yourself—free from the automatic patterns that no longer serve your life.

Preparing for the Deep Work

Understanding the lasting impact of your childhood experiences prepares you for the healing work ahead. The next chapters will help you identify your parent's specific personality disorder and understand how it shaped your particular adaptations. This specificity matters because different disorders create different impacts, requiring different healing approaches.

You're not broken, and you don't need to be fixed. You're a person who adapted brilliantly to difficult circumstances and now has the opportunity to update those adaptations for a life of greater freedom and authenticity.

Key Insights

- **Attachment patterns** formed with personality-disordered parents become templates for adult relationships, influencing trust, intimacy, and emotional safety
- **Neurobiological changes** from chronic childhood stress create lasting effects on emotional regulation, decision-making, and threat assessment

- **Common adult symptoms** like anxiety, depression, and relationship difficulties represent logical adaptations to illogical family systems
- **Complex PTSD** develops from ongoing relational trauma rather than specific incidents, affecting core identity and relationship capacity
- **Childhood survival strategies** that once protected you may now interfere with adult thriving, creating the need for conscious pattern updates
- **Neuroplasticity offers hope**—the same brain flexibility that adapted to childhood challenges can also support adult healing and growth

Chapter 4: The Dramatic Cluster - When Emotions Rule

The emergency room was busy that Tuesday night, but the woman's voice cut through the general din with theatrical precision. "My daughter is clearly having an allergic reaction, and no one seems to care!" she announced to anyone within hearing range. The triage nurse glanced at the chart—the daughter had a minor rash, already evaluated and treated. But the mother continued her performance, gesturing dramatically about medical negligence while her embarrassed teenage daughter sank deeper into her chair.

Dr. Susan Chen, working her shift, recognized the scene immediately. She'd grown up with similar performances from her own mother, whose emotions dominated every family situation. As an adult physician, she could see the histrionic pattern clearly in this parent-child dynamic. What struck her wasn't the mother's behavior—it was the teenager's response. The girl was expertly managing her mother's emotions, offering reassurance and redirection with the skill of a trained therapist.

This is Cluster B in action: the dramatic, emotional, erratic personality disorders that turn family life into an ongoing soap opera where children learn to manage adult emotions before they've learned to understand their own.

Understanding Cluster B: The Emotional Tornado

Cluster B personality disorders share several key features: emotional dysregulation, identity disturbances, and interpersonal difficulties. Parents with these disorders experience emotions intensely and have trouble regulating them effectively. Their feelings become the family's primary organizing principle, requiring everyone else to adjust their behavior to manage the parent's emotional state.

Children in these families learn that emotions are powerful, unpredictable forces that can overwhelm everything else. They become experts at reading emotional cues and adjusting their behavior to maintain stability. But they often struggle to understand and regulate their own emotions because they've been focused on managing everyone else's.

The four Cluster B disorders create different flavors of emotional chaos, but all of them teach children that relationships are intense, unpredictable, and centered around managing crisis.

Borderline PD: Living on an Emotional Rollercoaster

Borderline Personality Disorder involves severe emotional instability, intense fear of abandonment, and unstable relationships that alternate between idealization and devaluation. Parents with BPD experience emotions like a thermostat stuck on high—every feeling registers at crisis level.

The BPD Parent's Internal Experience:

BPD parents genuinely suffer. Their emotions feel overwhelming and uncontrollable. They experience criticism as devastating attacks and minor disappointments as complete rejections. Their fear of abandonment is so intense that they may become clingy and demanding, yet their emotional volatility often pushes others away, confirming their worst fears.

They desperately want close relationships but lack the emotional regulation skills to maintain them consistently. Love feels dangerous because it makes them vulnerable to the abandonment they fear most.

How BPD Affects Parenting:

- **Emotional instability creates chaos**: The parent's mood becomes the family weather system, with everyone adjusting their behavior based on Mom or Dad's emotional state
- **Fear of abandonment leads to enmeshment**: The parent may treat the child as their primary emotional support, making the child responsible for the parent's wellbeing

- **Black-and-white thinking affects relationships**: The child is either "all good" (when meeting the parent's needs) or "all bad" (when asserting independence)
- **Identity disturbance affects modeling**: The parent can't provide a stable sense of self for the child to learn from

Case Example: Maya's BPD Mother

Maya learned to read her mother's emotional barometer before she could read books. A bright smile meant it might be a good day—or it might mean Mom was manic and would crash later. A frown could indicate anything from minor irritation to suicidal ideation. Maya's childhood was spent walking on emotional eggshells, never knowing which version of Mom she'd encounter.

When Maya got accepted to college three hours away, her mother's response was explosive. "You're abandoning me just like everyone else!" she sobbed. "I knew you didn't really love me." The acceptance letter became evidence of Maya's selfishness rather than cause for celebration. Maya found herself comforting her mother and considering local schools instead.

Now 26, Maya struggles with her own emotional regulation. She either feels nothing at all or everything at once. Relationships terrify her because she learned that love means taking responsibility for someone else's emotional stability. She's attracted to intense, dramatic partners because calm relationships feel "boring" or "fake"—she doesn't trust affection that isn't accompanied by crisis.

Maya also battles with identity confusion. She learned to become whatever version of herself would best serve her mother's emotional needs. The cheerleader when Mom needed validation. The caretaker when Mom felt suicidal. The best friend when Mom felt lonely. She became so skilled at emotional chameleon work that she lost track of her authentic self.

The Parentification Dynamic:

BPD parents often reverse the parent-child relationship, making the child responsible for emotional caretaking. This "parentification" teaches children that love means sacrificing your own needs to manage someone else's emotions.

Signs of parentification include:

- Being told you're "mature for your age" or "the only one who understands"
- Feeling responsible for your parent's mood and wellbeing
- Learning to suppress your own needs to avoid upsetting your parent
- Being asked to mediate conflicts between adults
- Receiving inappropriate emotional confidences about adult problems

Histrionic PD: Life as Performance Art

Histrionic Personality Disorder involves excessive emotional expression, attention-seeking behavior, and discomfort when not the center of attention. Parents with HPD experience life as a continuous performance where they need to be the star.

The HPD Parent's Internal Experience:

HPD parents feel invisible and worthless when they're not receiving attention and admiration. Their self-worth depends entirely on external validation. They genuinely believe their dramatic presentations of emotion because feelings and facts blur together in their experience. They're not intentionally manipulative—they truly need the attention and validation to feel real.

How HPD Affects Parenting:

- **Attention competition**: The parent competes with the child for attention and admiration
- **Emotional hijacking**: The child's experiences get overshadowed by the parent's dramatic reactions

- **Performance pressure**: The child learns that ordinary experiences aren't worthy of attention
- **Boundary violations**: The parent treats the child as an audience member rather than a separate person with individual needs

Case Example: Jonathan's HPD Father

Jonathan's father was the life of every party and the star of every story. When Jonathan scored a goal in soccer, Dad's celebration was so over-the-top that other parents stared. What should have been Jonathan's moment of pride became Dad's performance about what an amazing father he was to have such a talented son.

When Jonathan struggled in math class, Dad transformed it into a dramatic story about the educational system failing gifted children. Parent-teacher conferences became Dad's opportunity to charm and impress rather than focus on Jonathan's actual needs. Even Jonathan's childhood illnesses became performances—Dad would post elaborate social media updates about his devotion as a caregiver, complete with photos of himself looking martyred while holding medicine.

Now 30, Jonathan struggles with a persistent sense that his life isn't interesting enough. Normal achievements feel meaningless unless they can generate drama and attention. He finds himself exaggerating stories to make them more compelling, then feeling like a fraud. He's successful professionally but can't enjoy quiet accomplishments because they don't feel "real" without external validation.

Jonathan also battles with authentic emotional expression. He learned that feelings only mattered if they were performed dramatically enough to earn attention. He can access theatrical emotional displays but struggles to recognize and express genuine emotions at normal volumes.

Narcissistic PD: Love With Conditions

Narcissistic parents create family systems organized around their grandiose self-image and need for admiration. Children learn that love is conditional on reflecting well on the parent and meeting the parent's image of what they should be.

The NPD Parent's Internal Experience:

Despite their outward confidence, narcissistic parents have fragile self-esteem that requires constant reinforcement. They genuinely believe they're special and deserving of admiration, but this belief is defended against underlying shame and inadequacy. They can't consistently see others as separate individuals with their own needs and feelings.

How NPD Affects Parenting:

- **Conditional love**: Affection and approval depend on the child meeting the parent's expectations
- **Identity control**: The parent decides who the child should be rather than supporting who they are
- **Empathy deficits**: The parent struggles to understand the child's separate emotional experience
- **Achievement pressure**: The child's accomplishments reflect on the parent's worth, creating intense performance pressure

Case Example: Lauren's NPD Mother

Lauren's mother loved having a daughter—as long as Lauren reflected well on her parenting. Lauren was enrolled in piano lessons, dance classes, and advanced academic programs not based on her interests, but on how her achievements would make Mom look to other parents.

When Lauren excelled, Mom took credit. "She gets her musical talent from me," she'd announce proudly. When Lauren struggled or showed interest in activities Mom didn't value, the response was cold disapproval. "I'm disappointed in you," became Lauren's most feared phrase because it meant the withdrawal of affection until she got back on track.

Lauren learned that love came with performance requirements. She excelled academically and professionally but never felt secure in relationships because she expected affection to be withdrawn if she failed to meet others' expectations. She struggles with perfectionism and people-pleasing, always scanning for signs that she's not measuring up.

Most challenging for Lauren is learning to identify and honor her own preferences. She became so skilled at figuring out what others wanted from her that she lost touch with her own desires and opinions. Decision-making feels impossible because she's not sure what she actually wants beyond what will earn approval.

Antisocial PD: When Empathy Is Missing

Antisocial Personality Disorder involves disregard for others' rights, lack of empathy, and manipulative behavior. Parents with ASPD view relationships as transactions and people as objects to be used for personal gain.

The ASPD Parent's Internal Experience:

ASPD parents don't experience empathy or guilt the way others do. They understand intellectually that others have feelings, but they don't feel emotionally moved by others' pain or joy. They're often charming and intelligent, able to mimic emotional responses they've learned are expected. Their primary motivations are personal gain and avoiding consequences.

How ASPD Affects Parenting:

- **Exploitation**: The child becomes a tool for meeting the parent's needs rather than a person to be nurtured
- **Manipulation training**: The child learns that relationships involve manipulation and that people are either useful or obstacles
- **Moral confusion**: The child receives inconsistent or harmful messages about right and wrong

- **Emotional neglect**: The parent can't provide genuine emotional attunement or support

Case Example: David's ASPD Father

David's father was charming, intelligent, and completely lacking in empathy. He taught David to lie convincingly by age eight, presenting it as a useful life skill. "People are either smart enough to avoid being fooled or they deserve what they get," he'd say with a smile.

Dad involved David in small cons and schemes, making it feel like exciting adventures rather than illegal activities. He taught David to read people's weaknesses and exploit them, to charm adults into giving him what he wanted, and to view kindness as weakness to be taken advantage of.

When David's pet died, his father's response was practical: "It's just a dog. We'll get another one if you want." When David cried, Dad called him weak and told him to "toughen up." David learned that emotions were vulnerabilities to be hidden and that caring about others was foolish.

Now 32, David struggles with authentic relationships. He automatically assesses what people want from him and adjusts his personality accordingly, but he's not sure how to simply be genuine. He knows intellectually that manipulation is wrong, but it's the relationship style he learned. He wants to be different but finds authentic connection confusing and uncomfortable.

David also battles with moral decision-making. His father's lessons created confusion about right and wrong that persists into adulthood. He second-guesses his moral instincts and struggles to trust his own judgment about ethical situations.

The Common Thread: Emotional Survival Training

Despite their differences, all Cluster B disorders teach children similar survival skills:

1. **Hypervigilance to emotions**: Reading others' moods becomes essential for physical and emotional safety
2. **Emotional caretaking**: Managing adults' feelings becomes the child's responsibility
3. **Identity flexibility**: Becoming whoever the parent needs them to be to maintain stability
4. **Crisis management**: Learning to function during emotional storms and dramatic events
5. **Manipulation detection and deployment**: Understanding how emotions can be used as tools

These skills often translate into adult strengths—many children of Cluster B parents become excellent therapists, negotiators, salespeople, or leaders because they learned to read and influence others expertly. But the same skills can create problems in personal relationships where authenticity and emotional regulation are more important than crisis management.

Exercises: Pattern Identification and Emotional Flashback Log

Pattern Identification Exercise:

For each type of dramatic parent, note whether these patterns feel familiar:

Borderline Patterns:

- [ ] Walking on eggshells around your parent's moods
- [ ] Feeling responsible for your parent's emotional wellbeing
- [ ] Being told you're "abandoning" them when you try to become independent
- [ ] Experiencing your parent as loving and rejecting, sometimes within the same day
- [ ] Being asked to comfort your parent when they were upset

Histrionic Patterns:

- [ ] Your achievements being overshadowed by your parent's dramatic reactions
- [ ] Feeling like you had to compete with your parent for attention
- [ ] Your parent making themselves the center of your experiences
- [ ] Learning that normal emotions weren't dramatic enough to be valid
- [ ] Your parent performing their parental role rather than simply being present

Narcissistic Patterns:

- [ ] Love feeling conditional on meeting your parent's expectations
- [ ] Your parent taking credit for your achievements
- [ ] Being told who you should be rather than supported for who you were
- [ ] Your parent's image being more important than your actual needs
- [ ] Feeling like a reflection of your parent rather than your own person

Antisocial Patterns:

- [ ] Being taught that people are either useful or obstacles
- [ ] Learning manipulation as a normal relationship skill
- [ ] Your parent lacking empathy for your pain or others' suffering
- [ ] Moral lessons that justified harmful behavior
- [ ] Feeling like a tool for your parent's goals rather than a child to be nurtured

Emotional Flashback Log:

Emotional flashbacks occur when current situations trigger childhood survival responses. Track these for a week to identify patterns:

When the flashback occurred: Date, time, situation

Physical sensations: Racing heart, tension, nausea, etc.

Emotional response: Panic, rage, numbness, overwhelm

Thoughts during the flashback: What stories was your mind telling you?

Childhood connection: What similar situation or feeling does this remind you of?

Age you felt: How old did you feel during the flashback?

Recovery time: How long did it take to feel normal again?

Look for triggers that activate your childhood emotional survival systems. Common triggers include criticism, conflict, having to wait for attention, or being asked to manage someone else's emotions.

The Path Through Drama

Growing up with Cluster B parents teaches intense emotional skills that can become either strengths or obstacles in adult life. The key is learning when these skills serve you and when they interfere with the life you want to create.

Your hypervigilance to emotions might make you an excellent friend and partner—or it might exhaust you with constant monitoring of others' moods. Your crisis management skills might make you invaluable professionally—or they might leave you creating drama when life feels too calm. Your ability to read and influence others might make you a natural leader—or it might prevent you from forming authentic relationships.

The healing journey involves keeping the strengths while learning new skills for situations that don't require emotional survival tactics. You don't need to eliminate your emotional intelligence—you need to gain conscious control over when and how you use it.

Transitioning to Calm

The next chapter explores a very different type of disordered parenting: Cluster C, the anxious and fearful disorders. Where Cluster B parents create chaos through emotional intensity, Cluster C parents create problems through rigid control and fearful restriction. Understanding both extremes helps you recognize how different types of dysfunction create different adaptations—and require different healing approaches.

Key Insights

- **Cluster B disorders** create emotional chaos where children learn to manage adult feelings before understanding their own
- **Borderline parents** teach children that love means emotional caretaking and that relationships involve constant crisis management
- **Histrionic parents** compete with children for attention, teaching that ordinary experiences aren't worthy of notice
- **Narcissistic parents** provide conditional love based on performance, teaching that worth must be earned through achievement
- **Antisocial parents** lack empathy and teach manipulation as normal relationship behavior
- **Emotional flashbacks** occur when current situations trigger childhood survival responses, revealing patterns that need conscious updating
- **Survival skills** learned in dramatic families can become adult strengths when used consciously rather than automatically

Chapter 5: The Anxious Cluster - When Fear Controls

The family restaurant was nearly empty on a Tuesday evening, but eight-year-old Emma's father insisted they sit in the corner booth facing the entrance. "You never know who might come in," he muttered, scanning each new arrival with suspicious eyes. When the waitress approached with a smile, Dad's posture stiffened. "She's being too friendly. She probably wants a bigger tip."

Emma learned to see the world through her father's lens of constant vigilance and mistrust. By age ten, she could spot "suspicious" behavior in strangers and felt anxious in social situations her friends navigated easily. What felt like protection was actually training in a worldview where danger lurked around every corner and other people couldn't be trusted.

This is Cluster C in action: the anxious, fearful personality disorders that create family environments dominated by worry, control, and rigid rules designed to manage ever-present threats—most of which exist only in the parent's mind.

Understanding Cluster C: When Safety Becomes Prison

Cluster C disorders share common themes of anxiety, fear, and rigid attempts to control environments to feel safe. Unlike Cluster B parents who create chaos through emotional drama, Cluster C parents create problems through excessive control and fearful restriction.

These parents genuinely want to protect their children, but their own anxiety creates family systems organized around avoiding perceived threats. Children learn that the world is dangerous, that they can't handle challenges independently, and that safety comes through rigid adherence to rules and expectations.

The three Cluster C disorders create different flavors of anxious control, but all teach children that autonomy is dangerous and that security comes through dependence or perfect compliance.

Avoidant PD: The Art of Emotional Distance

Avoidant Personality Disorder involves social inhibition, feelings of inadequacy, and hypersensitivity to negative evaluation. Parents with AvPD protect themselves from rejection by avoiding deep connections, including with their own children.

The AvPD Parent's Internal Experience:

AvPD parents desperately want connection but are terrified of rejection and criticism. They feel inadequate and assume others will eventually reject them once they see their flaws. Social situations feel dangerous because they might expose their perceived inadequacies. They interpret neutral interactions as potentially critical and withdraw to protect themselves.

They love their children but struggle to express that love in ways children can receive because emotional expression feels risky and vulnerable.

How AvPD Affects Parenting:

- **Emotional distance**: The parent provides practical care but avoids emotional intimacy
- **Social isolation**: The family becomes isolated from community connections
- **Criticism sensitivity**: The parent models extreme sensitivity to any form of evaluation
- **Risk avoidance**: The child learns that trying new things leads to potential humiliation

Case Example: Robert's AvPD Mother

Robert's mother was physically present but emotionally invisible. She attended his school events but sat in the back, leaving immediately after. She provided excellent meals, clean clothes, and transportation to activities, but conversations stayed focused on logistics and schedules.

When Robert tried to share excitement about friendships or achievements, Mom responded with brief acknowledgments before changing the subject to practical matters. When he faced social problems or disappointments, she offered solutions ("Maybe you should just avoid those kids") rather than emotional support or encouragement to work through difficulties.

Mom's own social anxiety was contagious. She worried about what other parents thought, avoided school volunteer opportunities, and rarely invited people to their home. Robert learned that social connections were sources of potential judgment rather than joy and support.

Now 29, Robert struggles with emotional intimacy. He can maintain friendly relationships but feels lost when conversations turn to deeper emotional territory. He intellectually knows that people form close bonds, but the mechanics feel foreign. Dating is particularly challenging because he doesn't know how to express or receive romantic affection authentically.

Robert also battles with social anxiety inherited from his mother. He assumes others are evaluating him critically and avoids situations where he might be judged. Professional networking feels impossible, limiting his career growth. He wants connection but fears the vulnerability it requires.

Dependent PD: The Enmeshment Trap

Dependent Personality Disorder involves excessive need to be taken care of, leading to submissive and clinging behavior. Parents with DPD reverse the normal parent-child dependency, making the child responsible for meeting the parent's needs for care and support.

The DPD Parent's Internal Experience:

DPD parents feel helpless and incompetent when facing life's challenges. They genuinely believe they can't handle difficulties independently and need someone stronger to guide and support them. They experience normal adult responsibilities as overwhelming and look for others to make decisions for them.

When they become parents, they often turn to their children to meet these dependency needs, creating role-reversed relationships where children become caregivers.

How DPD Affects Parenting:

- **Role reversal**: The child becomes the emotional caretaker for the parent
- **Decision avoidance**: The parent asks the child to make age-inappropriate choices
- **Anxiety transmission**: The parent's helplessness creates anxiety in the child about their own competence
- **Boundary confusion**: The parent treats the child as a peer or support system rather than a developing person

Case Example: Lisa's DPD Father

Lisa's father was overwhelmed by adult responsibilities and turned to her for emotional support from an early age. When bills arrived, he'd show them to eight-year-old Lisa and ask, "What do you think we should do?" When he had conflicts with coworkers, he'd seek Lisa's advice about how to handle the situation.

Dad presented these conversations as treating Lisa "like an adult," but they actually burdened her with anxiety about problems she couldn't solve. She learned to comfort him when he felt overwhelmed, to help him make decisions, and to manage his emotional states. She became hyperresponsible while he remained dependent.

The role reversal extended to practical matters. Lisa learned to cook, manage schedules, and handle correspondence because Dad found these tasks "too stressful." She felt proud of her competence but also resentful of the burden.

Now 35, Lisa attracts partners who need caretaking and feels uncomfortable when others try to support her. She's professionally successful because she learned early to handle responsibilities others avoid, but she struggles to receive care or admit her own needs. Relaxation feels selfish because someone might need her help.

Lisa also battles with decision-making paralysis in areas where she wasn't parentified. While she can manage crises and support others expertly, she feels lost when making choices about her own happiness and desires. She learned to anticipate others' needs but not to identify her own.

Obsessive-Compulsive PD: The Perfectionism Prison

Obsessive-Compulsive Personality Disorder involves preoccupation with orderliness, perfectionism, and control. Parents with OCPD create family systems organized around rigid rules and impossible standards where love feels conditional on perfect compliance.

The OCPD Parent's Internal Experience:

OCPD parents genuinely believe that there's a "right way" to do everything and that deviation from these standards leads to disaster. They feel anxious and out of control when things don't meet their exact specifications. They see their perfectionism as helpful and can't understand why others find their standards burdensome.

They want their children to succeed and believe that high standards are the path to achievement and happiness. They can't see how their impossible expectations create anxiety and self-doubt.

How OCPD Affects Parenting:

- **Conditional love**: Affection depends on meeting the parent's standards for behavior and achievement
- **Perfectionism pressure**: "Good enough" never actually qualifies as acceptable

- **Rigid control**: Deviation from the parent's methods is seen as defiance or incompetence
- **Micromanagement**: The parent controls details that should be left to the child's discretion

Case Example: Sarah's OCPD Mother

Sarah's mother had detailed systems for everything. Homework required three drafts minimum, with Mom reviewing each version and providing extensive feedback. Sarah's bedroom faced daily inspection with points deducted for dust, improperly folded clothes, or books not aligned perfectly on shelves.

Love came with performance reviews—literally. Mom kept charts tracking Sarah's grades, chores, and behavior, with privileges and affection dispensed based on scores. A 92% on a test led to analysis of what went wrong and how to improve next time. A messy backpack became a character flaw requiring correction.

Family vacations involved detailed itineraries planned months in advance, with every activity scheduled and contingency plans for weather or delays. Spontaneity was seen as poor planning. Fun activities had to serve educational or self-improvement purposes to be worthwhile.

Now 31, Sarah struggles with decision paralysis because no choice feels perfectly correct. She rewrites emails multiple times before sending them, double-checks work that's already excellent, and feels anxious about any situation that might be evaluated. Success brings no satisfaction because there's always room for improvement.

Sarah also battles with self-compassion. She inherited her mother's inner critic, which constantly evaluates her performance and finds it lacking. She can extend kindness to others but feels that accepting her own mistakes or limitations would make her weak or complacent.

The Common Thread: Fear-Based Control

Despite their differences, all Cluster C disorders teach children that the world is threatening and that safety comes through rigid control or avoidance:

1. **Hypervigilance to criticism**: Constantly monitoring for signs of disapproval or rejection
2. **Avoidance of risk**: Learning that trying new things leads to potential failure or humiliation
3. **External validation dependence**: Needing others' approval to feel secure
4. **Perfectionism as protection**: Believing that perfect performance prevents rejection
5. **Emotional suppression**: Learning that feelings create vulnerability and should be controlled

These adaptations often create adults who are responsible, reliable, and high-achieving, but who struggle with anxiety, decision-making, and authentic self-expression.

The Perfectionism Spectrum

OCPD creates a particularly damaging form of perfectionism that goes beyond healthy striving for excellence. Understanding the difference helps identify whether your standards serve you or imprison you.

Healthy Striving:

- Standards are high but achievable
- Mistakes are seen as learning opportunities
- Success brings satisfaction and pride
- Worth isn't dependent on performance
- "Good enough" is sometimes acceptable

Perfectionist Prison:

- Standards are impossible to meet consistently
- Mistakes feel catastrophic and shameful
- Success brings only temporary relief before the bar gets raised
- Worth depends entirely on flawless performance
- "Good enough" never actually qualifies

Signs You're Trapped in Perfectionism:

- Spending excessive time on tasks that others complete quickly
- Difficulty delegating because others won't do it "right"
- Procrastination due to fear of imperfect results
- All-or-nothing thinking about performance
- Physical symptoms of stress when facing evaluation

Exercise: Boundary Assessment

Cluster C families often struggle with healthy boundaries because anxiety makes parents either overprotective (rigid boundaries) or dependent (collapsed boundaries). This exercise helps identify your current boundary patterns.

Emotional Boundaries:

- Do you feel responsible for others' feelings?
- Can you maintain your own emotional state when others are upset?
- Do you take on others' problems as if they were your own?
- Can you say no to requests that drain your energy?

Physical Boundaries:

- Are you comfortable with appropriate physical affection?
- Do you respect others' need for physical space?
- Can you ask for physical space when you need it?
- Do you feel entitled to privacy about your body and belongings?

Time Boundaries:

- Can you prioritize your own schedule and commitments?
- Do you feel guilty taking time for rest or recreation?
- Are you able to be unavailable when necessary?
- Do you feel compelled to be productive at all times?

Decision Boundaries:

- Can you make choices based on your own values and preferences?
- Do you seek excessive input from others before deciding?
- Are you able to disagree with people you care about?
- Do you feel confident in your judgment about your own life?

Communication Boundaries:

- Can you express disagreement respectfully?
- Are you able to keep appropriate information private?
- Do you feel compelled to justify your choices to others?
- Can you listen to criticism without becoming defensive or devastated?

For areas where boundaries feel difficult, notice the fears that arise. Common fears include abandonment, criticism, making mistakes, or being seen as selfish. These fears often connect directly to messages received from anxious parents.

Exercise: Perfectionism Scale

Rate each statement from 1 (never) to 5 (always):

1. I have trouble finishing projects because they're never quite right
2. I feel stressed when I can't control how things are done
3. I notice flaws that others seem to miss or ignore
4. I feel like a failure when I make mistakes others consider minor

5. I work much longer than necessary to get things "perfect"
6. I feel uncomfortable when my living or work space isn't organized exactly right
7. I have difficulty delegating because others don't meet my standards
8. I procrastinate on tasks where I might not excel
9. I feel anxious when facing any kind of evaluation
10. I believe that anything worth doing must be done perfectly

Scoring:

- 10-22: Healthy striving with manageable standards
- 23-35: Moderate perfectionism that may cause some stress
- 36-50: High perfectionism likely interfering with wellbeing and relationships

Higher scores often correlate with OCPD parenting, but perfectionism can develop from any anxiety-based family system.

Breaking Free from Fear-Based Living

The challenge for adult children of Cluster C parents is learning to distinguish between reasonable caution and anxiety-driven avoidance, between healthy standards and perfectionist prison, between appropriate consideration and excessive people-pleasing.

Key Healing Tasks:

1. **Updating threat assessment**: Learning to distinguish between real dangers and anxiety-based fears
2. **Developing distress tolerance**: Building capacity to handle imperfection, uncertainty, and criticism
3. **Practicing authentic self-expression**: Learning to share thoughts and feelings even when they might not be perfectly received
4. **Building self-compassion**: Treating yourself with the kindness you'd show a good friend

5. **Experimenting with "good enough"**: Deliberately practicing less-than-perfect performance in low-stakes situations

The Gifts Hidden in Anxiety

Many adult children of anxious parents develop remarkable strengths:

- **High conscientiousness**: Reliability and attention to detail that others value
- **Risk assessment skills**: Ability to anticipate problems and plan accordingly
- **Empathy for others' struggles**: Understanding what it feels like to be overwhelmed or inadequate
- **Strong work ethic**: Willingness to put in effort to achieve goals
- **Loyalty and commitment**: Deep investment in relationships and responsibilities

The healing journey isn't about eliminating these qualities but about gaining conscious choice over when to use them. Your conscientiousness might make you an excellent employee—but it shouldn't prevent you from taking vacation time. Your risk assessment might help you make wise financial decisions—but it shouldn't stop you from trying new experiences that could bring joy.

Case Study: Integration and Growth

Let's revisit Robert, whose avoidant mother taught him that emotional connection was dangerous. His healing journey illustrates how Cluster C adaptations can be updated rather than eliminated.

Robert began therapy feeling frustrated with his social isolation but terrified of vulnerability. His therapist helped him understand that his emotional caution made sense given his childhood experience, but that adult relationships offered different risks and rewards than his mother had encountered.

Starting with small steps, Robert practiced emotional expression in low-risk situations. He shared minor frustrations with coworkers, expressed genuine appreciation to friends, and gradually increased his emotional vocabulary. He discovered that most people responded positively to authentic connection rather than judging him as his mother had feared.

Robert also learned to distinguish between his mother's social anxiety and his own social preferences. He realized he genuinely enjoyed quieter social activities and didn't need to become extroverted to have meaningful relationships. He could honor his introverted nature while still building the connections he craved.

The breakthrough came when Robert recognized that his cautious approach to relationships, while limiting, also had benefits. He was thoughtful about others' feelings, careful not to intrude on their boundaries, and deeply loyal to those who earned his trust. These qualities, when balanced with appropriate vulnerability, made him a valued friend and partner.

Preparing for Complexity

The next chapter explores an even more challenging territory: when parents have multiple personality disorders or when both parents have disorders. These complex family systems create layered adaptations that require careful unraveling to understand.

But first, take a moment to acknowledge the courage it takes to examine these patterns. Growing up with anxious, controlling parents often creates adults who are highly self-critical and reluctant to recognize their own strength. You survived a childhood that taught you the world was dangerous and that you couldn't trust your own judgment. Yet here you are, reading this book and working to understand your experience. That takes remarkable resilience and wisdom.

Key Insights

- **Cluster C disorders** create family environments dominated by anxiety, rigid control, and fearful restriction of normal childhood experiences
- **Avoidant parents** teach emotional distance as safety, leaving children skilled at practical care but struggling with intimacy and emotional expression
- **Dependent parents** reverse normal roles, making children responsible for adult emotional and decision-making needs
- **OCPD parents** create perfectionism prisons where love is conditional on meeting impossible standards, teaching children that worth must be earned through flawless performance
- **Fear-based control** teaches hypervigilance, risk avoidance, and external validation dependence as survival strategies
- **Perfectionism** becomes problematic when standards are impossible to meet and mistakes feel catastrophic rather than educational
- **Boundary difficulties** arise when anxiety makes parents either overprotective or inappropriately dependent on their children
- **Hidden strengths** often develop from anxious backgrounds—conscientiousness, empathy, reliability—that can be assets when used consciously rather than compulsively

Chapter 6: The Eccentric Cluster - When Reality Shifts

The grocery store checkout line was moving normally until the woman ahead of them started talking to the cashier about surveillance cameras. "They're not just for shoplifting," she whispered urgently. "They're collecting facial recognition data for the government database. That's why I always wear sunglasses indoors." She glanced around suspiciously, including at twelve-year-old Kevin and his mother, who were simply trying to buy milk and bread.

Kevin's stomach tightened with familiar embarrassment and confusion. This was his life—constant vigilance for threats that seemed invisible to everyone else, elaborate explanations for normal situations, and the gnawing sense that he was either missing something crucial or that his mother was seeing things that weren't there.

This is Cluster A in action: the odd, eccentric personality disorders that create family environments where reality itself becomes uncertain and children learn to navigate a world where their parent's perceptions don't match what others see.

Understanding Cluster A: When Normal Becomes Strange

Cluster A personality disorders share common features of unusual thinking, social withdrawal, and behavior that others find odd or eccentric. Unlike Cluster B's emotional drama or Cluster C's anxious control, Cluster A creates confusion about reality itself.

Parents with these disorders often have difficulty distinguishing between their internal experiences and external reality. They may see connections where none exist, interpret neutral events as meaningful, or withdraw so completely from social interaction that their children learn to do the same.

Children in these families face a unique challenge: learning to trust their own perceptions while living with a parent whose reality doesn't match the outside world. They often become skilled at code-switching between their family's version of reality and the version they encounter everywhere else.

Paranoid PD: Living Under Siege

Paranoid Personality Disorder involves pervasive distrust and suspicion of others, interpreting benign actions as malevolent. Parents with PPD create family environments organized around defending against threats that may exist only in their minds.

The PPD Parent's Internal Experience:

PPD parents genuinely believe they're surrounded by people who wish them harm. They interpret coincidences as conspiracies, kindness as manipulation, and normal social behavior as evidence of hidden agendas. Their hypervigilance feels necessary for survival because they experience the world as genuinely dangerous.

They love their children but express that love through protective measures that often isolate the family from normal social experiences. They're teaching survival skills for a hostile world as they perceive it.

How PPD Affects Parenting:

- **Isolation from community**: The parent limits the child's exposure to "dangerous" outside influences
- **Hypervigilance training**: The child learns to scan for threats and question others' motives
- **Reality distortion**: The child receives explanations for normal events that don't match others' interpretations
- **Trust issues**: The child learns that most people can't be trusted and have hidden agendas

Case Example: Maria's PPD Father

Maria's father saw threats everywhere. The friendly neighbor was "clearly gathering intelligence about our family." Her teachers' interest in her welfare was "suspicious—why do they care so much about what happens at home?" Even extended family members were viewed with distrust because "blood doesn't guarantee loyalty."

Family life revolved around defensive measures. They had multiple locks on doors, security cameras, and detailed protocols for who could be trusted with what information. Dad kept detailed records of interactions with others, looking for patterns that confirmed his suspicions. Maria learned to notice who was watching them in public and to report unusual behavior from classmates or teachers.

When Maria made friends at school, Dad's response was interrogative: "What do you know about their family? Why are they interested in being your friend? What do they ask about our family?" Innocent childhood friendships became potential security breaches requiring investigation.

Now 28, Maria struggles with trusting her own judgment about people. Part of her knows that Dad's level of suspicion was excessive, but she can't completely shake the habit of looking for hidden motives in others' behavior. Dating is particularly challenging because romantic interest feels inherently suspicious—why would someone want to get close to her unless they had ulterior motives?

Maria also battles with social anxiety rooted in hypervigilance. She automatically scans social situations for signs of threat or deception, making relaxed social interaction difficult. She wants to believe that most people are basically good, but her nervous system stays alert for danger signals her father taught her to recognize.

Schizoid PD: The Art of Emotional Invisibility

Schizoid Personality Disorder involves detachment from social relationships and restricted emotional expression. Parents with SPD provide physical care but remain emotionally absent, creating family environments where feelings are neither expressed nor acknowledged.

The SPD Parent's Internal Experience:

SPD parents don't experience the drive for social connection that motivates most people. They're not avoiding relationships because they fear rejection—they genuinely don't feel the need for emotional intimacy. They may love their children in their way, but that love doesn't translate into emotional warmth or engagement.

They often find emotional expressions from others puzzling or overwhelming and prefer interactions that stay focused on practical matters rather than feelings.

How SPD Affects Parenting:

- **Emotional desert**: The family environment lacks emotional warmth, sharing, or connection
- **Isolation modeling**: The child learns that withdrawal is normal and that emotional needs are unreasonable
- **Limited social learning**: The child doesn't learn emotional vocabulary or interpersonal skills
- **Self-reliance pressure**: The child learns early that emotional support isn't available and must be self-sufficient

Case Example: Alex's SPD Mother

Alex's mother was physically present but emotionally invisible. She provided excellent practical care—nutritious meals, clean clothes, transportation to activities—but emotional connection was absent. Conversations focused on logistics: schedules, homework, household tasks. When Alex tried to share excitement about achievements or concerns about problems, Mom listened politely and offered brief, practical responses before returning to her tasks.

Family time was spent in parallel activities rather than interactive ones. They might sit in the same room, but Mom would read while Alex played, with minimal interaction. Television shows or movies that required emotional engagement were avoided in favor of documentaries or news programs that could be discussed intellectually.

When Alex faced typical childhood challenges—friendship drama, disappointment about not making a team, anxiety about tests—Mom's response was consistently practical. "Have you talked to the teacher about extra credit?" or "Maybe you should find different friends." Emotional support or validation for feelings wasn't part of the equation.

Now 30, Alex struggles with emotional intimacy in all relationships. He intellectually understands that people form deep emotional bonds, but the experience feels foreign. He's attracted to partners but doesn't know how to create or maintain emotional closeness. Physical affection feels awkward, and conversations about feelings seem pointless or indulgent.

Alex also battles with emotional awareness in himself. He can identify major emotions like anger or sadness, but the subtle variations and complex feelings that others navigate easily are mysterious to him. He functions well professionally because work relationships don't require emotional depth, but personal relationships feel like a foreign language he was never taught.

Schizotypal PD: When Thinking Gets Weird

Schizotypal Personality Disorder involves acute discomfort with close relationships, cognitive distortions, and eccentric behavior. Parents with STPD create family environments where unusual thinking patterns are normalized and reality becomes fluid.

The STPD Parent's Internal Experience:

STPD parents experience reality differently than most people. They may see meaningful connections between unrelated events, believe they have special insights or abilities, or interpret coincidences as messages. Their thinking patterns feel normal and logical to them, even when others find them bizarre.

They often feel different from other people and may believe they have special knowledge or abilities that others lack. This can create a sense of superiority mixed with social alienation.

How STPD Affects Parenting:

- **Reality confusion**: The child receives explanations for events that don't match conventional understanding
- **Social alienation**: The family becomes isolated due to the parent's eccentric behavior and beliefs
- **Magical thinking**: The child learns to see connections and meanings that may not exist
- **Identity confusion**: The child struggles to distinguish between normal and abnormal thinking patterns

Case Example: Jordan's STPD Mother

Jordan's mother lived in a world of hidden meanings and special connections. She believed that certain numbers appearing repeatedly were messages from the universe about important decisions. She interpreted dreams as prophetic and made family plans based on their symbolic content. When Jordan got sick, Mom would analyze what spiritual lesson the illness was meant to teach rather than simply providing comfort and medical care.

Mom had elaborate theories about energy fields, electromagnetic sensitivity, and psychic abilities that she believed ran in their family. Jordan learned to interpret physical sensations as spiritual messages and to look for signs and omens in daily events. Normal coincidences became evidence of cosmic intervention or warning signs about future events.

Social interactions were filtered through Mom's unusual worldview. She believed she could sense people's "true nature" through their energy and would make decisions about Jordan's friendships based on her psychic impressions rather than on the children's actual behavior. Some families were deemed "spiritually compatible" while others were viewed as having "negative vibrations."

Now 26, Jordan struggles with distinguishing between intuition and paranoid thinking. She sometimes catches herself looking for hidden meanings in random events or making decisions based on "signs" rather than practical considerations. She knows intellectually that some of her mother's beliefs were delusional, but she can't completely shake the feeling that there might be truth in them.

Jordan also battles with social integration. She learned to hide her family's eccentric beliefs from outsiders, becoming skilled at code-switching between her home reality and social reality. This created a persistent sense of being fake or deceptive, even when she was simply adapting to different social environments.

The Common Thread: Reality Distortion

All Cluster A disorders create families where normal social reality is distorted:

1. **Hypervigilance to threats** (paranoid) or **emotional withdrawal** (schizoid) or **magical connections** (schizotypal)
2. **Social isolation** from community norms and relationships
3. **Reality testing difficulties** distinguishing between accurate and distorted perceptions
4. **Trust confusion** about whether to believe their own perceptions or others'
5. **Code-switching skills** between family reality and social reality

These adaptations often create adults who are highly observant and independent but who struggle with social connection and reality testing in ambiguous situations.

Exercise: Reality Testing Worksheet

This exercise helps you practice distinguishing between accurate perceptions and anxiety-driven interpretations. For situations that trigger suspicion or concern, work through these questions:

The Situation: Describe what actually happened in objective, observable terms.

Your Initial Interpretation: What story did your mind immediately create about this situation?

Evidence For Your Interpretation: What concrete evidence supports this interpretation?

Evidence Against Your Interpretation: What evidence suggests other possible explanations?

Alternative Explanations: What are three other possible explanations for what happened?

Most Likely Explanation: Based on available evidence, what's the most probable explanation?

Action Based on Evidence: What action, if any, does the evidence actually support?

Practice this process with minor situations first—someone not responding to a text, a coworker seeming distant, a friend canceling plans. Build your skill at separating observable facts from interpretive stories before applying it to more emotionally charged situations.

Exercise: Social Skills Inventory

Cluster A families often provide limited modeling for normal social interaction. This inventory helps identify areas where you might benefit from conscious skill development:

Conversation Skills:

- Can you make small talk comfortably?
- Are you able to share appropriate personal information?
- Do you ask others questions about their experiences and interests?

- Can you express disagreement without becoming confrontational?

Emotional Expression:

- Are you comfortable expressing positive emotions like excitement or affection?
- Can you share vulnerable emotions like sadness or fear when appropriate?
- Do you recognize and respond to others' emotional cues?
- Are you able to offer comfort when others are distressed?

Social Boundaries:

- Can you recognize when others need space or privacy?
- Are you able to ask for space when you need it?
- Do you share information appropriate to the level of relationship?
- Can you maintain friendships without becoming enmeshed or isolated?

Conflict Resolution:

- Are you able to address problems directly rather than avoiding them?
- Can you apologize when you've made mistakes?
- Do you know how to compromise and find middle ground?
- Are you able to forgive others for minor offenses?

Group Dynamics:

- Can you participate in group conversations without dominating or disappearing?
- Are you comfortable with the natural flow of group attention?
- Do you contribute appropriately to group decisions?
- Can you handle being the focus of positive attention?

Areas where skills feel underdeveloped often reflect limited modeling in your family of origin. These skills can be learned in adulthood through conscious practice and, if needed, professional support.

The Unique Challenge of Cluster A Recovery

Healing from Cluster A backgrounds involves a particularly complex challenge: learning to trust your own perceptions while updating the distorted reality testing you may have inherited.

Unlike Cluster B recovery (which focuses on emotional regulation) or Cluster C recovery (which focuses on anxiety management), Cluster A recovery requires rebuilding your relationship with reality itself. This involves:

Developing Accurate Reality Testing: Learning to distinguish between accurate perceptions, anxiety-driven interpretations, and inherited distortions from your family system.

Building Social Skills: Consciously learning interpersonal skills that others absorbed naturally through family modeling.

Managing Inherited Suspicion: Learning when caution is appropriate versus when it's driven by inherited paranoid thinking patterns.

Connecting Without Losing Yourself: Building relationships while maintaining the independence and self-reliance that helped you survive your family environment.

The Hidden Gifts of Eccentric Families

Despite their challenges, Cluster A families often produce adults with remarkable strengths:

- **Independent thinking**: Ability to question conventional wisdom and form original opinions

- **Observational skills**: Heightened awareness of subtle social and environmental cues
- **Self-reliance**: Comfort with solitude and ability to function independently
- **Creativity**: Unconventional thinking patterns that can lead to innovation
- **Authenticity**: Less concern with social conformity, more willingness to be genuine

The healing journey isn't about becoming "normal" in a conventional sense, but about gaining conscious choice over when to use these gifts and when to adapt to social expectations.

Integration and Growth

Let's revisit Maria, whose paranoid father taught her to see threats everywhere. Her recovery journey illustrates how Cluster A adaptations can be updated while preserving their beneficial aspects.

Maria began therapy feeling exhausted by constant hypervigilance but afraid to lower her guard. Her therapist helped her understand that her father's level of suspicion, while excessive, had taught her valuable observational skills that served her well professionally.

Working gradually, Maria practiced distinguishing between reasonable caution and paranoid fear. She learned to gather evidence before assuming negative intent, to consider multiple explanations for ambiguous behavior, and to take calculated social risks despite feeling vulnerable.

The breakthrough came when Maria realized that her careful approach to relationships, while limiting, also protected her from genuinely problematic people. She was skilled at reading social dynamics and recognizing manipulation—skills that many people lack. She could honor this ability while also learning to trust appropriate people appropriately.

Maria didn't need to become naive or careless to heal. She needed to gain conscious control over her threat assessment system, using it when genuinely helpful while overriding it when it interfered with the connections she wanted to build.

Preparing for Complexity

The next chapter explores what happens when families have multiple personality disorders operating simultaneously, or when both parents have different disorders. These complex systems create layered adaptations that require careful analysis to understand and address.

Understanding single disorders provides the foundation, but many families operate with multiple overlapping patterns that create unique challenges. The child must adapt not just to one type of dysfunction, but to contradictory demands from different disorders operating in the same family system.

Key Insights

- **Cluster A disorders** create family environments where reality itself becomes uncertain, requiring children to navigate contradictory perceptions of normal situations
- **Paranoid parents** teach hypervigilance and suspicion as survival skills, creating children who struggle to trust their own judgment about others' motivations
- **Schizoid parents** provide practical care without emotional connection, leaving children skilled at independence but struggling with intimacy and emotional expression
- **Schizotypal parents** normalize unusual thinking patterns and magical connections, creating confusion about what constitutes normal versus eccentric thought processes
- **Reality testing difficulties** arise when family explanations for events don't match outside world interpretations, requiring conscious skill development in adulthood
- **Social isolation** is common across Cluster A families, limiting children's exposure to normal relationship modeling and social skill development

- **Code-switching abilities** develop from needing to adapt between family reality and social reality, creating valuable observational skills alongside authenticity challenges
- **Hidden strengths** from eccentric backgrounds include independent thinking, keen observation skills, self-reliance, and authentic self-expression when conscious choices replace automatic patterns

Chapter 7: Mixed Messages - When Multiple Disorders Collide

The family meeting was supposed to address Jenny's declining grades, but within minutes it had devolved into familiar chaos. Her borderline mother was sobbing about being a failure as a parent while her narcissistic father lectured about the importance of excellence, occasionally pausing to comfort his wife with theatrical displays of support. Meanwhile, her obsessive-compulsive grandmother (who lived with them) was reorganizing Jenny's homework folder and muttering about how proper organization would solve everything.

Jenny sat in the middle of this dysfunction sandwich, trying to simultaneously manage her mother's emotional crisis, meet her father's performance demands, and satisfy her grandmother's organizational requirements. At fifteen, she was already developing the complex skill set required to navigate multiple personality disorders operating in the same family system.

This is the reality for millions of children: growing up not with one clear pattern of dysfunction, but with contradictory demands from multiple disordered family members. These complex systems create adaptive challenges that go far beyond what single-disorder families face.

When Disorders Multiply

Research from PubMed Central and Cambridge studies shows that personality disorders frequently co-occur, both within individuals and within families. Some combinations are particularly common:

- **Borderline + Narcissistic**: Emotional volatility combined with grandiose entitlement
- **Avoidant + Dependent**: Social fear combined with excessive need for support
- **Paranoid + Obsessive-Compulsive**: Suspicious hypervigilance combined with rigid control

- **Antisocial + Narcissistic**: Lack of empathy combined with grandiose self-importance

When multiple disorders exist in one parent, children face contradictory messages and constantly shifting expectations. When both parents have different disorders, children must navigate entirely different rule systems depending on which parent they're interacting with.

Case Example: The Borderline-Narcissistic Parent

Rachel's mother embodied both borderline and narcissistic patterns in a toxic combination that created impossible double-binds. During her narcissistic phases, Mom demanded that Rachel be exceptional—the smartest student, the most talented performer, the perfect daughter who reflected well on her superior parenting. Love came with achievement requirements and constant comparison to other children who "weren't as special as you."

But during borderline episodes, those same achievements became threats. When Rachel excelled academically, Mom would have emotional breakdowns about being "abandoned by her own daughter who thinks she's too good for her family now." Success in activities Mom had pushed her toward became evidence that Rachel was "growing away from me and becoming like everyone else who eventually leaves."

Rachel learned to hide her achievements during Mom's fragile periods and to emphasize them during her demanding phases. She developed hypervigilance not just to emotional cues, but to which personality disorder was currently dominant. The skills required were contradictory: grandiose confidence for the narcissistic parent versus emotional caretaking for the borderline episodes.

Now 32, Rachel struggles with imposter syndrome and achievement anxiety that reflect both disorder influences. She simultaneously craves recognition (narcissistic training) and fears that success will lead to abandonment (borderline training). She can't enjoy achievements because they trigger both grandiose expectations and abandonment fears.

Case Example: The Two-Disorder Household

Michael grew up with an obsessive-compulsive father and an avoidant mother—a combination that created a household organized around rigid rules and emotional distance. Dad's OCPD demanded perfect compliance with detailed systems for everything from homework to household chores. Every task had a correct method, and deviation was seen as defiance or incompetence.

Mom's avoidant patterns meant she provided practical support for Dad's systems but no emotional connection or warmth. When Michael struggled with the impossible standards, he received correction but no comfort. When he succeeded in meeting Dad's requirements, he received approval but no genuine celebration or emotional connection.

The combination taught Michael that love came through perfect performance of rigid tasks, but that emotional expression of that love wasn't part of the equation. He learned to derive satisfaction from meeting impossible standards while expecting no emotional reward for his efforts.

Michael excelled academically and professionally because he could meet demanding requirements without needing emotional support. But relationships felt foreign because he'd learned to connect through task completion rather than emotional sharing. He attracts partners who appreciate his competence but then feels lonely within those relationships because emotional intimacy feels impossible.

Substance Abuse: The Complicating Factor

Family Intervention research shows that personality disorders and substance abuse frequently co-occur, creating additional layers of complexity. The substance use often represents an attempt to self-medicate the distress caused by the personality disorder, but it adds unpredictability and additional trauma to the family system.

How Substances Complicate Personality Disorders:

- **Inconsistent presentations**: The parent's behavior varies not just based on their disorder, but on their level of intoxication
- **Doubled dysfunction**: Children must navigate both the personality disorder patterns and addiction-related behaviors
- **Trauma layering**: Physical and emotional abuse often increase during active addiction periods
- **Hope and disappointment cycles**: Periods of sobriety may temporarily improve functioning, creating false hope followed by devastating relapses

Case Example: Borderline + Alcoholism

Sarah's mother had borderline personality disorder complicated by alcoholism—a combination that created extreme unpredictability. Sober Mom was emotionally volatile but generally loving. She might have crying episodes about feeling abandoned, but she'd also have periods of intense connection where Sarah felt genuinely cherished.

Drunk Mom was dangerous. The emotional dysregulation that characterized her borderline patterns became violent when combined with alcohol. She'd rage about perceived slights, threaten suicide over minor disappointments, and occasionally become physically aggressive when her abandonment fears peaked.

Sarah learned to assess not only Mom's emotional state but also her level of intoxication. The same trigger could result in tears (sober borderline), verbal abuse (mildly drunk borderline), or physical violence (severely drunk borderline). Sarah developed complex assessment skills that went far beyond normal emotional attunement.

The addiction also created hope and disappointment cycles that complicated Sarah's relationship with both recovery and her mother. During Mom's periodic sober periods, Sarah would dare to hope that family life could be stable. But relapses were inevitable, creating repeated trauma around attachment and loss.

Navigating Contradictory Demands

Children in multi-disorder families become skilled at code-switching between different behavioral requirements depending on which disorder is currently dominant or which parent they're interacting with. This creates valuable adaptability skills but also identity confusion and chronic stress.

Common Contradictory Messages:

Narcissistic vs. Borderline Parent:

- "Be exceptional and independent" vs. "Don't abandon me"
- "You're special and superior" vs. "You're all I have"
- "Achieve great things" vs. "Don't grow away from me"

OCPD vs. Avoidant Parent:

- "Meet my detailed standards" vs. "Don't expect emotional connection"
- "Perfection is required" vs. "Feelings are unnecessary"
- "Engage with my systems" vs. "Maintain emotional distance"

Paranoid vs. Dependent Parent:

- "Trust no one" vs. "I need you to take care of me"
- "Be hypervigilant" vs. "Make decisions for me"
- "People are dangerous" vs. "I can't handle being alone"

These contradictions create children who are highly adaptable but chronically confused about their authentic identity and needs.

Both Parents with Disorders

When both parents have personality disorders, children face the additional challenge of having no stable reference point within the family system. Normal families have at least one parent who can provide reality testing and emotional regulation. Multi-disorder families may lack any consistent source of stability.

Case Example: Narcissistic Father + Avoidant Mother

Lisa grew up with a narcissistic father who demanded constant admiration and performance, and an avoidant mother who withdrew from emotional engagement entirely. Dad required Lisa to be his audience and admirer—praising his achievements, listening to his stories, and reflecting his grandiose self-image. Mom provided practical care but no emotional warmth or connection.

The combination taught Lisa that relationships involved either performing for others' egos or maintaining distant self-sufficiency. She learned to be charming and engaging (to meet Dad's needs) while remaining emotionally disconnected (like Mom). Love was either a performance or an absence—nothing in between felt familiar.

Lisa became successful professionally because she could charm colleagues and clients while maintaining professional boundaries. But intimate relationships felt impossible because she'd never experienced the middle ground between narcissistic supply and avoidant distance. She either performed for partners or withdrew from them, unable to access authentic emotional reciprocity.

Exercise: Family Dynamics Mapping

This exercise helps you visualize the complex patterns in your family system and understand how different disorders interacted to create contradictory demands.

Step 1: Identify the Disorders List each family member and their likely personality disorder patterns (if any). Include both parents, grandparents, siblings, or other household members who significantly influenced your development.

Step 2: Map the Contradictions For each combination of disorders in your household, identify the contradictory messages you received:

- What did Parent A require from you?
- What did Parent B require from you?
- How were these requirements incompatible?
- What happened when you couldn't meet both simultaneously?

Step 3: Identify Your Adaptations How did you learn to navigate these contradictions?

- Which skills did you develop to manage multiple demands?
- How did you decide which parent's needs to prioritize when they conflicted?
- What parts of yourself did you learn to hide or suppress?
- What survival strategies did you develop?

Step 4: Recognize Current Patterns How do these childhood adaptations show up in your adult life?

- Do you still code-switch between different behavioral styles?
- Are you attracted to people who recreate familiar disorder patterns?
- Do you feel confused about your authentic identity or preferences?
- Are you skilled at managing others' contradictory needs?

Step 5: Assess the Impact What are the costs and benefits of your adaptations?

- Which skills serve you well in adult situations?
- Which patterns now interfere with your wellbeing or relationships?
- What aspects of yourself feel authentic versus performative?
- Where do you want to make conscious changes?

The Adaptation Advantages

While multi-disorder families create significant challenges, they also often produce adults with remarkable skills:

Advanced Emotional Intelligence: Reading complex emotional dynamics and adapting behavior accordingly

Crisis Management: Functioning effectively during chaos and managing multiple urgent demands simultaneously

Flexibility: Adapting communication and behavior styles to different people and situations

Independence: Functioning without consistent external support or validation

Problem-Solving: Finding creative solutions to complex interpersonal challenges

Empathy: Understanding multiple perspectives and adapting to others' needs

These skills often translate into professional success in fields requiring interpersonal sophistication—therapy, sales, management, diplomacy, or crisis intervention.

The Identity Challenge

The most significant long-term impact of multi-disorder families is often identity confusion. When you've spent your childhood adapting to contradictory demands from multiple disordered parents, authentic self-expression can feel foreign and dangerous.

Common Identity Issues:

- **Chameleon syndrome**: Being so skilled at becoming what others need that you lose touch with your authentic self
- **Choice paralysis**: Having difficulty making decisions because you're unsure what you actually want versus what would meet others' needs

- **Relationship confusion**: Being attracted to people who recreate familiar dysfunction because healthy relationships feel boring or fake
- **Imposter feelings**: Feeling like you're performing life rather than authentically living it
- **Value uncertainty**: Having difficulty identifying your own values separate from what you learned to value to survive

Healing the Fragmented Self

Recovery from multi-disorder families requires a different approach than single-disorder healing. Instead of updating one set of adaptive patterns, you need to integrate multiple adaptations and choose consciously which to keep, which to modify, and which to replace.

Key Healing Tasks:

1. **Identify all your adaptations**: Recognize the different behavioral styles you learned for different family members
2. **Assess current usefulness**: Determine which adaptations serve you well and which interfere with your goals
3. **Develop authentic preferences**: Practice identifying what you want independent of what others need
4. **Choose conscious responses**: Select behaviors based on current situations rather than childhood survival patterns
5. **Integrate your skills**: Combine the best aspects of your various adaptations into a coherent sense of self

The Path to Integration

Jenny, from our opening example, eventually learned to see her complex adaptation skills as strengths rather than evidence of being "fake" or "confused." Her childhood had taught her to read emotional dynamics expertly, to adapt her communication style effectively, and to manage multiple demands simultaneously.

In therapy, she learned to distinguish between healthy adaptation (adjusting your communication style for different professional contexts) and survival adaptation (constantly monitoring others' needs to avoid conflict). She kept the skills that served her well while learning to access her authentic preferences and needs.

The goal wasn't to become a single, static personality, but to gain conscious choice over her various capabilities. She could be the skilled crisis manager when the situation required it, the empathetic supporter when others needed comfort, or the firm boundary-setter when her own needs required protection.

Preparing for the Developmental View

Understanding how multiple disorders interact provides the foundation for our next exploration: how these complex family dynamics affect children differently depending on their developmental stage. The same dysfunctional family system creates different impacts on a toddler versus an adolescent, requiring different healing approaches based on when the major disruptions occurred.

The next chapter examines how personality-disordered parenting affects development from infancy through young adulthood, helping you understand not just what happened in your family, but when it happened and how those timing factors continue to influence your adult functioning.

Key Insights

- **Multiple disorders** in families create contradictory demands that require complex adaptation skills, often producing adults with remarkable interpersonal abilities alongside identity confusion
- **Common combinations** like borderline + narcissistic or OCPD + avoidant create specific double-bind situations where meeting one parent's needs violates another's requirements
- **Substance abuse complications** add unpredictability and additional trauma layers to personality disorder patterns, creating hope-disappointment cycles around addiction recovery

- **Both parents with disorders** eliminates stable reference points within the family, requiring children to develop external reality testing and emotional regulation skills independently
- **Code-switching abilities** develop from navigating different behavioral requirements for different family members, creating valuable adaptability alongside authentic identity challenges
- **Advanced emotional intelligence** often develops from managing complex family dynamics, translating into professional strengths in interpersonally demanding fields
- **Identity integration** becomes a primary healing task, requiring conscious choice over which adaptations to maintain versus modify for current life goals
- **Healing approaches** must address multiple adaptation patterns simultaneously rather than focusing on single-disorder recovery strategies

Chapter 8: Through a Child's Eyes - Developmental Impact

Three-year-old Emma stood on her tiptoes to reach the kitchen counter, carefully arranging crackers on a plate. Her mother hadn't eaten all day—again—and was lying on the couch staring at the ceiling with that empty look that meant she'd disappeared somewhere inside herself. Emma had learned that bringing food sometimes helped Mommy come back, even though she couldn't understand why grown-ups forgot to eat when her stomach reminded her constantly.

At three, Emma was already developing adaptations that would shape her entire life trajectory. Her brain was learning that adults couldn't be counted on for basic needs, that she was responsible for others' wellbeing, and that emotional attunement meant scanning for signs of psychological absence rather than connection.

The impact of personality-disordered parenting varies dramatically based on the child's developmental stage when the major disruptions occur. Understanding these developmental differences helps explain why some aspects of your adult functioning feel more damaged than others and why certain healing approaches work better for your particular pattern of strengths and struggles.

The Developing Brain Under Stress

Research from the National Child Traumatic Stress Network and Cambridge studies shows that chronic stress during key developmental windows creates lasting changes in brain architecture and functioning. The earlier and more severe the disruption, the more fundamental the adaptive changes become.

Key Developmental Principles:

- **Sequential development**: Later stages build on earlier foundations, so disruptions early in development affect all subsequent stages

- **Critical periods**: Certain capacities develop during specific windows; missed opportunities may require more intensive intervention later
- **Neuroplasticity**: The brain remains changeable throughout life, but early patterns become deeply ingrained and automatic
- **Attachment as foundation**: Early relationship patterns create templates that influence all future relationships

Understanding your developmental timeline helps identify which capacities developed normally versus which were disrupted, providing a roadmap for targeted healing work.

Infancy (0-18 months): The Foundation of Trust

During infancy, children develop their most basic understanding of whether the world is safe and whether they are worthy of care. This stage involves fundamental attachment formation and early nervous system regulation.

What Healthy Infancy Provides:

- Secure attachment through consistent, responsive caregiving
- Nervous system co-regulation through attuned parental response
- Basic trust in others' reliability and goodwill
- Foundation for emotional regulation and self-soothing
- Sense of being inherently worthy of love and care

How Personality Disorders Disrupt Infancy:

Borderline parents during infancy create inconsistent caregiving based on their emotional state. The baby may receive intense attention during the parent's good periods but neglect during emotional crises. This teaches the infant that care is unpredictable and depends on factors beyond their control.

Narcissistic parents may provide excellent physical care but limited emotional attunement if the baby's needs don't align with their self-image as perfect parents. Crying or fussiness may be interpreted as criticism of their parenting rather than normal infant communication.

Avoidant parents often provide consistent physical care but limited emotional responsiveness. The baby learns that emotional needs go unmet while practical needs are handled efficiently.

Case Example: Attachment Disruption in Infancy

Marcus's borderline mother experienced severe postpartum depression combined with her existing emotional volatility. Some days she was intensely focused on Marcus, holding him constantly and responding immediately to every cry. Other days, she felt overwhelmed and couldn't tolerate his needs, leaving him to cry while she isolated herself.

By six months, Marcus had learned to be a "good baby"—crying minimally, entertaining himself, and accepting care from whoever was available. His early nervous system adapted to unpredictable caregiving by becoming hypervigilant and self-soothing.

Now 28, Marcus struggles with relationships that require consistent emotional presence. He's excellent in crisis situations because he learned early to function without reliable support, but ongoing intimacy feels foreign. He either clings anxiously (when activated by abandonment fears) or withdraws completely (when overwhelmed by connection needs).

Early Childhood (18 months - 5 years): Identity Formation

During early childhood, children develop their sense of self as separate individuals with their own thoughts, feelings, and preferences. This stage involves learning emotional regulation, developing language for feelings, and beginning to understand social relationships.

What Healthy Early Childhood Provides:

- Support for developing autonomy while maintaining connection
- Emotional vocabulary and regulation skills through modeling and teaching
- Recognition and validation of the child's separate identity
- Safe exploration of independence and individual preferences
- Understanding that feelings are temporary and manageable

How Personality Disorders Disrupt Early Childhood:

OCPD parents during this stage often cannot tolerate the mess and chaos that normal development creates. The child's natural exploration and experimentation get controlled and corrected, preventing normal learning about cause and effect, personal preferences, and emotional expression.

Histrionic parents may compete with the child for attention during this stage, unable to allow the child to be the center of age-appropriate situations. The child learns that their experiences only matter if they generate sufficient drama and attention.

Antisocial parents may begin teaching manipulation during this stage, praising the child for charming behaviors while modeling exploitation of others' emotions and needs.

Case Example: Identity Formation Disruption

Jennifer's histrionic mother couldn't tolerate Jennifer's natural developmental assertion of preferences and independence. When three-year-old Jennifer said "No, I want to wear the red dress," Mom interpreted this as rejection and launched into theatrical distress about Jennifer "not loving Mommy anymore."

Jennifer learned that asserting preferences caused devastating emotional reactions in the person she depended on most. She adapted by becoming hyperattuned to Mom's emotional needs and suppressing her own preferences to maintain the relationship.

Now 30, Jennifer struggles with decision-making and authentic self-expression. She automatically scans others' reactions when making choices and feels anxious about asserting preferences that might disappoint or upset others. Her early identity formation was hijacked by the need to manage her mother's emotions.

School Age (6-11 years): Competence and Social Learning

During school age, children develop skills, learn about themselves in social contexts, and begin comparing themselves to peers. This stage involves building competence, forming friendships, and developing more sophisticated emotional understanding.

What Healthy School Age Provides:

- Opportunities to develop competence and mastery in various areas
- Social skill development through peer interaction
- Reality testing through exposure to different family systems
- Academic learning that builds confidence and capability
- Recognition of individual strengths and interests

How Personality Disorders Disrupt School Age:

Paranoid parents may limit the child's social exposure during this crucial period, preventing normal peer relationship development and reality testing. The child misses opportunities to learn that not all families operate with suspicion and hypervigilance.

Dependent parents may interfere with normal competence development by continuing to handle tasks the child should be learning independently. The child doesn't develop normal self-efficacy and confidence in their abilities.

Case Example: Social Learning Disruption

David's paranoid father severely limited his social interactions during elementary school. Playdates required extensive background checks on other families. After-school activities were viewed as potential security risks. David learned that social connections were dangerous and that his family's vigilant approach was necessary for survival.

David missed crucial peer relationship development during the primary socialization period. He didn't learn normal social skills, conflict resolution, or friendship maintenance because his exposure was so limited. His social anxiety as an adult stems partly from missing these foundational learning experiences.

Adolescence (12-18 years): Identity Integration and Independence

Adolescence involves integrating childhood experiences into a coherent identity and beginning the process of separation from family. This stage includes identity exploration, values development, and preparation for adult independence.

What Healthy Adolescence Provides:

- Support for identity exploration and values development
- Gradual increase in independence and responsibility
- Recognition of the adolescent as a separate individual with their own path
- Emotional support during the natural turbulence of this developmental stage
- Preparation for adult relationships and responsibilities

How Personality Disorders Disrupt Adolescence:

BPD parents often cannot tolerate normal adolescent separation and may escalate their emotional demands or threats during this stage. The teenager learns that independence equals abandonment and that their natural developmental drives cause devastating pain to those they love.

NPD parents may view adolescent identity exploration as defiance if it doesn't align with their vision for the child. The teenager learns that authentic self-expression threatens the relationship and that love requires conforming to others' expectations.

Case Example: Independence Disruption

Sarah's borderline mother interpreted every normal adolescent independence behavior as abandonment. When Sarah wanted to spend time with friends instead of family, Mom accused her of "growing away from the family." When Sarah expressed interest in colleges far from home, Mom had suicidal episodes that required Sarah's caretaking attention.

Sarah learned that her natural developmental drives toward independence were dangerous to her mother's wellbeing. She suppressed normal adolescent identity exploration to maintain family stability, never fully developing her own sense of direction and values.

Young Adulthood (18-25 years): Launching and Intimacy

Young adulthood involves completing the separation from family of origin and beginning to form intimate adult relationships. This stage includes career development, romantic partnerships, and fully autonomous decision-making.

What Healthy Young Adulthood Provides:

- Support for complete independence while maintaining family connection
- Recognition of the young adult as a separate individual with their own life path
- Models for healthy intimate relationships and partnerships
- Encouragement for career and personal goal development
- Gradual shift from parent-child to adult-adult relationship

How Personality Disorders Disrupt Young Adulthood:

This stage often activates the most severe responses from personality-disordered parents because it represents the ultimate threat to their control or enmeshment with the child. The young adult may face intense guilt, manipulation, or emotional blackmail for pursuing normal developmental goals.

Case Example: Launch Disruption

Lisa's OCPD father couldn't tolerate her making independent decisions about career and relationships during her early twenties. Every choice she made that didn't align with his detailed plans for her life was treated as evidence of poor judgment requiring his intervention.

When Lisa chose to study art instead of business, Dad launched an extensive campaign to "help her see reason," including financial manipulation, academic research about career prospects, and lectures about responsibility. Lisa learned that independent decision-making created enormous conflict and that peace required conforming to others' standards.

Exercise: Timeline of Impact Activity

This exercise helps you identify which developmental stages were most disrupted in your family and how those timing factors continue to influence your adult functioning.

Step 1: Create Your Developmental Timeline

Draw a timeline from birth to age 25, marking major family events:

- When did your parent's disorder symptoms peak or improve?
- Were there periods of particular crisis or stability?
- When did substance abuse, mental health crises, or major life changes occur?
- How did your parent's behavior change as you moved through different stages?

Step 2: Identify Stage-Specific Impacts

For each developmental stage, note:

Infancy (0-18 months):

- Was caregiving consistent and responsive?
- Do you have information about your early attachment patterns?
- Were there major disruptions (hospitalization, depression, family crises)?

Early Childhood (18 months - 5 years):

- Were you encouraged to explore and express preferences?
- How were your emotions responded to and managed?
- Did you learn emotional vocabulary and regulation skills?

School Age (6-11 years):

- Were you allowed normal peer interactions and friendships?
- Could you develop competence in areas of interest?
- Did you have reality testing through exposure to other families?

Adolescence (12-18 years):

- Were you supported in identity exploration and values development?
- Could you express disagreement or different preferences?
- Was normal independence encouraged or discouraged?

Young Adulthood (18-25 years):

- Were you supported in making independent life choices?
- Could you pursue relationships and career goals freely?
- Did your family accept your adult autonomy?

Step 3: Connect Past to Present

For each stage where significant disruption occurred, identify current adult challenges:

- What capacities feel underdeveloped or damaged?
- Which situations trigger responses that seem disproportionate to current circumstances?
- Where do you feel like you're functioning from a younger developmental stage?

Step 4: Identify Strengths and Compensations

Also note areas where disruption led to early development of capabilities:

- What skills did you develop earlier than typical due to family needs?
- Which adaptive strategies serve you well in adult situations?
- How did you compensate for missing developmental experiences?

The Neurobiological Legacy

Each developmental stage disruption creates specific neurobiological adaptations that persist into adulthood:

Early disruption (infancy/early childhood) affects fundamental systems:

- Basic trust and safety assessment
- Emotional regulation and nervous system reactivity
- Attachment patterns and relationship templates
- Self-worth and identity formation

Later disruption (school age/adolescence) affects more sophisticated systems:

- Social skills and peer relationship capacity
- Identity integration and values development
- Independence and decision-making confidence
- Intimate relationship formation

Understanding your specific pattern helps explain why some aspects of adult functioning feel solid while others feel fragile or underdeveloped.

Healing Across Developmental Stages

Recovery often involves going back to complete interrupted developmental tasks:

Infancy repair: Learning to trust, developing self-soothing skills, building secure attachment patterns

Early childhood repair: Developing emotional vocabulary, learning healthy autonomy, practicing authentic self-expression

School age repair: Building social skills, developing competence, updating reality testing through new experiences

Adolescence repair: Exploring identity and values, practicing healthy separation, developing authentic preferences

Young adult repair: Building intimate relationship skills, making autonomous decisions, creating adult-to-adult family relationships

The good news is that neuroplasticity allows these repairs to happen in adulthood, though they may require conscious effort and often professional support.

Integration and Hope

Emma, from our opening example, eventually learned that her early adaptation of caretaking others wasn't her fault—it was brilliant survival strategy by a three-year-old brain trying to ensure her mother's survival and thus her own. Her healing journey involved appreciating the intelligence of her early adaptations while learning that adult relationships offered different possibilities.

She kept her ability to notice others' needs and offer appropriate support, but learned that she could also express her own needs and receive care from others. She didn't need to eliminate her caretaking instincts—she needed to gain conscious choice over when to use them.

Your developmental timeline provides a map for understanding why certain aspects of adult functioning feel natural while others feel impossible. The timing of disruptions creates the specific pattern of your strengths and challenges, pointing toward the healing work that will be most beneficial for your particular history.

Moving into Healing

Understanding your developmental experience provides the foundation for the healing journey ahead. The next section of this book focuses on recognizing current trauma patterns, learning evidence-based recovery approaches, and building the specific skills your developmental history indicates you need.

You survived disruptions that could have destroyed your capacity for growth and connection. The adaptations that helped you survive can be updated to help you thrive. Your journey toward wholeness honors both the child who adapted brilliantly to impossible circumstances and the adult who has the power to choose a different path forward.

Key Insights

- **Developmental timing** of personality disorder disruptions creates specific patterns of adult strengths and challenges, with earlier disruptions affecting more fundamental capacities
- **Infancy disruptions** affect basic trust, attachment security, and nervous system regulation, creating adult difficulties with consistent intimacy and emotional safety
- **Early childhood disruptions** interfere with identity formation and emotional regulation, leading to adult struggles with authentic self-expression and decision-making confidence

- **School age disruptions** limit social skill development and reality testing through peer interaction, creating adult social anxiety and relationship difficulties
- **Adolescence disruptions** prevent normal identity integration and independence development, leading to adult identity confusion and separation guilt
- **Young adulthood disruptions** interfere with launching and intimate relationship formation, creating adult struggles with autonomous decision-making and partnership skills
- **Neurobiological adaptations** from each developmental stage persist into adulthood but can be updated through conscious healing work and often professional support
- **Developmental repair** is possible throughout life due to neuroplasticity, involving conscious completion of interrupted developmental tasks appropriate to current life stage
- **Timeline mapping** helps identify which capacities need targeted healing work versus which developed normally and can serve as strengths in recovery

Chapter 9: Breaking the Spell - Recognizing Trauma Patterns

The meeting was supposed to be routine. Sarah had earned a promotion and her manager wanted to discuss her new responsibilities. But as she sat in the conference room, her heart raced like she was facing a firing squad. Her palms sweated. Her mind raced through every mistake she'd made in the past six months. When her manager smiled and said, "Congratulations, you've really earned this," Sarah's first thought wasn't pride—it was suspicion. What did he really want? What was the catch?

This is trauma talking. Not the dramatic, movie-version trauma of car crashes or natural disasters, but the quiet, persistent trauma of growing up with parents whose love came with impossible conditions, unpredictable moods, or emotional absence. Sarah's nervous system had learned in childhood that good news was often followed by criticism, that praise was a setup for higher expectations, and that letting her guard down meant getting hurt.

Twenty years after leaving her perfectionist mother's house, Sarah's body still carried the vigilant tension of a child who could never quite do enough to feel safe.

The Hidden Epidemic of Survival Responses

Research from the National Child Traumatic Stress Network shows that children who grow up with personality-disordered parents develop sophisticated coping mechanisms that help them survive impossible family dynamics. These aren't character flaws or personal weaknesses—they're brilliant adaptive strategies created by developing brains trying to maintain safety and attachment in chaotic environments.

The problem arises when these survival responses outlive their usefulness. The hypervigilance that protected you from your paranoid parent's unpredictable suspicions now makes normal workplace feedback feel threatening. The people-pleasing that prevented your borderline parent's abandonment rage now leaves you exhausted from constantly managing others' emotions. The emotional numbing that helped you survive your avoidant parent's coldness now interferes with intimate relationships.

Understanding these patterns isn't about judging yourself for having them—it's about recognizing how brilliantly you adapted and choosing which adaptations still serve your adult life versus which ones need updating.

Common Coping Mechanisms and Their Hidden Costs

The Hypervigilance Trap

Hypervigilance involves constantly scanning your environment for signs of danger, criticism, or disapproval. For children of personality-disordered parents, this vigilance often focused on reading the parent's emotional state to predict and prevent crisis.

You learned to notice micro-expressions that signaled your mother's mood was shifting toward rage. You developed radar for your father's tone changes that meant criticism was coming. You became an expert at reading between the lines, looking for hidden meanings, and preparing for emotional storms.

The cost of hypervigilance in adulthood is exhaustion. Your nervous system never fully relaxes because part of your attention is always scanning for threats. You notice things others miss—the slight tension in your partner's voice, the brief frown on your boss's face, the pause before your friend answers your question. But instead of feeling gifted with insight, you feel burdened with constant worry about what these signals might mean.

Case Example: Marcus and the Hypervigilance Burden

Marcus, now 34, grew up with a paranoid father who saw threats everywhere and taught Marcus to be equally vigilant. Dad's suspicions weren't entirely irrational—he'd experienced real betrayals in business and relationships—but his response was to teach Marcus that survival required constant wariness.

By age ten, Marcus could assess strangers' trustworthiness within minutes of meeting them. He noticed inconsistencies in people's stories, picked up on subtle signs of deception, and rarely felt surprised by others' behavior because he'd learned to expect the worst.

These skills served Marcus well in his career as a fraud investigator, but they made personal relationships nearly impossible. On dates, he automatically looked for signs that women were using him, lying to him, or planning to hurt him. Friends felt like he was constantly evaluating their motives rather than simply enjoying their company. Even positive interactions felt suspect—kindness might be manipulation, generosity might have strings attached.

Marcus's hypervigilance had protected him from some genuine threats over the years, but it also protected him from connection, trust, and joy. His nervous system couldn't distinguish between appropriate caution and inherited paranoia, so it defaulted to maximum alert at all times.

The People-Pleasing Prison

People-pleasing involves automatically prioritizing others' needs, emotions, and preferences over your own. For children of personality-disordered parents, this often developed as a strategy to maintain the parent's emotional stability and avoid conflict.

You learned that your parent's happiness was more crucial than your own comfort. You suppressed your preferences when they conflicted with your parent's needs. You became skilled at anticipating what others wanted and providing it before they even asked. You learned to find your worth through being useful, helpful, and accommodating.

The cost of people-pleasing in adulthood is losing yourself. You become so focused on making others happy that you lose track of your own needs, preferences, and boundaries. You attract people who take advantage of your accommodating nature while pushing away those who want genuine reciprocal relationships. You feel resentful but can't express it directly because conflict feels dangerous.

Case Example: Jennifer and the People-Pleasing Trap

Jennifer grew up with a histrionic mother whose emotional needs dominated every family situation. Mom required constant attention, validation, and emotional caretaking from everyone around her, but especially from Jennifer, who became her primary emotional support system.

Jennifer learned to read Mom's emotional barometer before she could read books. She knew which topics would trigger Mom's theatrical distress, which compliments would brighten her mood, and which behaviors would earn praise versus criticism. Jennifer's own needs became secondary to the family's primary goal of keeping Mom emotionally stable.

Now 31, Jennifer automatically adjusts her personality to match what others seem to want from her. With friends who value adventure, she becomes spontaneous and bold. With colleagues who appreciate reliability, she becomes steady and predictable. With romantic partners who seem to want nurturing, she becomes endlessly supportive and self-sacrificing.

The exhausting part isn't the adapting itself—Jennifer is genuinely skilled at reading others and responding to their needs. The problem is that she's lost touch with her authentic preferences and feelings underneath all the adaptation. She doesn't know what she actually likes, wants, or needs because she's been focused on what others need from her for so long.

The Emotional Numbing Defense

Emotional numbing involves disconnecting from feelings as a protection against overwhelming pain. For children of personality-disordered parents, this often developed when emotional expression was dangerous, unwelcome, or consistently invalidated.

You learned that crying made things worse, that anger brought punishment, that excitement led to disappointment. You developed the ability to turn off your feelings like a switch, to function through crisis without falling apart, to maintain composure when others were losing control.

The cost of emotional numbing in adulthood is disconnection from life's richness. You can handle crisis brilliantly but struggle to feel joy. You're reliable in emergencies but have trouble accessing passion or excitement. You've protected yourself from pain but also from pleasure, connection, and meaning.

Case Example: David and the Numbing Strategy

David's schizoid parents provided excellent practical care but no emotional warmth or connection. Feelings weren't discussed, acknowledged, or validated. When David experienced normal childhood emotions—excitement about achievements, sadness about disappointments, fear about challenges—his parents responded with practical solutions rather than emotional support.

David learned that emotions were private matters that shouldn't be shared and wouldn't be understood. He developed remarkable self-sufficiency and emotional control, handling problems independently and rarely bothering others with his feelings.

Now 35, David functions well professionally and maintains friendly relationships, but intimacy feels foreign. He can provide support to others but struggles to receive it. He intellectually understands that close relationships involve emotional sharing, but the mechanics feel uncomfortable and pointless. He's protected himself from emotional pain but also from emotional connection.

The Fawn Response Revolution

Recent research highlighted in Pete Walker's work on Complex PTSD has identified a fourth trauma response beyond fight, flight, or freeze: **fawn**. This response involves attempting to please or appease threats rather than fighting, escaping, or shutting down.

The fawn response is epidemic among adult children of personality-disordered parents because it often worked better than other strategies in these family systems. Fighting back against a narcissistic parent brought crushing retaliation. Running away wasn't possible when you were a child. Freezing led to being criticized for being unresponsive or difficult.

But fawning—becoming helpful, compliant, and accommodating—sometimes earned approval, reduced conflict, and maintained the attachment you needed for survival.

Signs of the Fawn Response:

- Automatically saying "sorry" even when you haven't done anything wrong
- Having difficulty expressing disagreement or setting boundaries
- Feeling responsible for others' emotions and moods
- Being attracted to people who need rescuing or fixing
- Feeling guilty when you prioritize your own needs
- Having trouble identifying your authentic preferences and opinions

The fawn response becomes problematic in adult relationships because it prevents genuine intimacy. Others never get to know the real you because you're constantly adjusting yourself to meet their needs. You never get to experience being loved for who you truly are because you're always performing who you think others want you to be.

Exercise: Coping Inventory

This exercise helps you identify which survival strategies you developed and how they currently affect your life. For each category, rate how frequently you experience these patterns on a scale of 1 (never) to 5 (constantly).

Hypervigilance Patterns:

- I notice micro-expressions and tone changes that others miss
- I automatically scan new environments for potential problems
- I have trouble relaxing because part of me is always alert
- I assume negative intentions when situations are ambiguous
- I feel responsible for predicting and preventing others' problems

People-Pleasing Patterns:

- I automatically prioritize others' needs over my own
- I have difficulty saying no to requests, even unreasonable ones
- I feel anxious when someone seems disappointed or upset with me
- I adjust my personality based on what I think others want
- I feel guilty when I do things purely for my own enjoyment

Emotional Numbing Patterns:

- I have trouble identifying what I'm feeling beyond "fine" or "stressed"
- I can handle crisis situations better than everyday emotional situations
- I feel like I'm watching my life from the outside rather than fully living it
- I have trouble crying even when I want to
- Others describe me as calm or composed when I feel empty inside

Fawn Response Patterns:

- I apologize frequently, even for things that aren't my fault
- I have difficulty expressing disagreement or conflicting opinions

- I feel responsible for managing others' emotional reactions
- I'm attracted to people who seem to need help or fixing
- I feel guilty when I assert my needs or boundaries

Scores of 15-20 in any category indicate significant patterns that may be interfering with your wellbeing and relationships. These aren't moral failings—they're evidence of how well you learned to survive difficult circumstances. Now you can choose which patterns still serve you and which ones you want to update.

Exercise: Trigger Identification

Triggers are situations that activate your childhood survival responses even when current circumstances don't require them. Identifying your triggers helps you respond consciously rather than reactively.

Common Trigger Categories for PD Survivors:

Authority Figures:

- Performance reviews or evaluations
- Being called into meetings without knowing the agenda
- Receiving feedback, even positive feedback
- Being asked to explain your choices or decisions

Interpersonal Conflicts:

- Someone seeming upset or disappointed
- Disagreements or different opinions being expressed
- Having to set boundaries or say no
- Feeling misunderstood or misinterpreted

Achievement Situations:

- Receiving recognition or praise
- Making mistakes or failing to meet standards
- Being the center of attention
- Having your competence questioned

Relationship Dynamics:

- Partners needing space or time alone
- Friends making plans without including you
- Changes in communication patterns or frequency
- Someone being busy or preoccupied

For each trigger you identify, note:

1. **Physical sensations:** How does your body respond?
2. **Emotional reaction:** What emotions arise immediately?
3. **Automatic thoughts:** What stories does your mind create?
4. **Childhood connection:** What similar situations did this remind you of?
5. **Behavioral response:** How do you typically react?

Understanding your triggers helps you pause between the activation and your response, creating space for conscious choice rather than automatic reaction.

The Perfectionism Paradox

Many adult children of personality-disordered parents develop perfectionism as a coping strategy, believing that flawless performance will finally earn the love, approval, or safety they craved in childhood.

Perfectionism feels productive because it often leads to high achievement and external recognition. But it's actually a trauma response—an attempt to control outcomes by eliminating any possibility of criticism or rejection.

Healthy Striving vs. Perfectionist Prison:

Healthy striving involves setting high standards while accepting that mistakes are part of learning and growth. Perfectionist prison involves setting impossible standards and experiencing any deviation as catastrophic failure.

Perfectionists often achieve a lot but can't enjoy their achievements because the focus immediately shifts to the next challenge or to finding flaws in their success. They work harder than necessary on tasks others would consider complete, struggle with delegation, and experience physical symptoms of stress around deadlines or evaluations.

The hidden cost of perfectionism is that it prevents authentic connection. Others feel like they have to be perfect around you too, or they feel inadequate compared to your impossible standards. You miss opportunities for genuine relationship because you're focused on maintaining your perfect image rather than being real.

Depression and Anxiety as Trauma Responses

Many adult children of personality-disordered parents experience depression and anxiety not as mental illness per se, but as natural responses to living with chronic stress and unmet developmental needs.

Trauma-Based Depression often involves:

- Feeling empty or disconnected rather than just sad
- Having difficulty accessing emotions or feeling "numb"
- Struggling with meaning and purpose
- Feeling like you're going through the motions of life
- Having trouble experiencing pleasure or satisfaction

Trauma-Based Anxiety often involves:

- Constant worry about others' reactions or approval
- Physical symptoms without clear medical causes
- Difficulty relaxing or "turning off" your mind
- Catastrophic thinking about normal life challenges
- Feeling responsible for outcomes beyond your control

Understanding these as trauma responses rather than personal defects helps you approach healing differently. Instead of just managing symptoms, you can address the underlying patterns that created them.

Breaking Free from Automatic Patterns

The first step in updating trauma responses is recognizing them without judgment. These patterns developed for good reasons and helped you survive circumstances that could have been devastating. The goal isn't to eliminate all your adaptive strategies—many of them are genuine strengths when used consciously rather than automatically.

Key Healing Principles:

1. **Notice without judgment:** Observe your patterns with curiosity rather than criticism
2. **Understand the logic:** Recognize how your responses made sense in their original context
3. **Assess current usefulness:** Determine which patterns serve your current life versus which interfere with your goals
4. **Practice conscious choice:** Create space between triggers and responses to choose your reaction
5. **Update gradually:** Make small changes rather than trying to transform everything at once

The next phase of your healing journey involves learning evidence-based therapeutic approaches that can help you process stored trauma, update maladaptive patterns, and build new skills for the life you want to create.

Bridging to Healing

Sarah, whose story opened this chapter, eventually learned to recognize her hypervigilance as a survival skill that had outlived its usefulness. She didn't eliminate her ability to read people and situations—that skill actually served her well in her leadership role. But she learned to distinguish between appropriate caution and inherited anxiety, using her observational abilities consciously rather than being controlled by them.

Your trauma patterns aren't evidence of weakness or damage—they're proof of your resilience and adaptability. Now you get to decide which aspects of your survival strategies to keep, which to modify, and which to replace with approaches better suited to the life you're creating.

Building Toward Solutions

Understanding your trauma patterns provides the foundation for exploring therapeutic approaches that can help you process stored experiences and develop new responses. The next chapter examines evidence-based treatments specifically effective for adult children of personality-disordered parents, helping you make informed decisions about your healing journey.

Key Takeaways

- **Trauma responses** from personality-disordered parenting include hypervigilance, people-pleasing, emotional numbing, and fawn responses that helped you survive but may now interfere with thriving
- **The fawn response** involves appeasing threats through compliance and accommodation, often becoming the primary survival strategy in PD families
- **Hypervigilance** creates exhaustion from constant threat-scanning while people-pleasing leads to losing authentic identity through excessive accommodation
- **Emotional numbing** protects from pain but also blocks joy and connection, while perfectionism attempts to control outcomes through impossible standards
- **Trigger identification** helps you recognize situations that activate childhood survival responses, creating space for conscious choice rather than automatic reaction
- **Depression and anxiety** often represent natural trauma responses to chronic stress rather than standalone mental health conditions

- **Healing involves** recognizing patterns without judgment, understanding their original logic, and consciously choosing which adaptations still serve your current life goals

Chapter 10: Therapeutic Approaches That Work

The therapist's office felt safe enough, but when Dr. Rodriguez asked Lisa to describe her childhood, the familiar wall went up immediately. "It wasn't that bad," Lisa heard herself say, the automatic response that had protected her for thirty-two years. "My parents had their issues, but they never hit me or anything. I had food, clothes, a roof over my head. Lots of people had it worse."

Dr. Rodriguez nodded thoughtfully. "And how did you feel about yourself as a child in that house?"

The question cracked something open. Lisa found herself crying for the first time in months, not from sadness exactly, but from recognition. She'd spent so much energy minimizing her experience that she'd never allowed herself to feel the impact of growing up with a mother whose emotional needs dominated every situation and a father whose rigid perfectionism made love feel like a performance review.

This is what effective therapy for adult children of personality-disordered parents looks like: creating space for experiences that were never allowed to be fully felt, witnessed, or validated.

Why Standard Therapy Often Misses the Mark

Traditional talk therapy approaches often fall short for adult children of personality-disordered parents because they weren't designed to address relational trauma or the complex adaptations these family systems create.

Cognitive Behavioral Therapy (CBT) focuses on changing thoughts and behaviors, but it may miss the deeper attachment wounds that drive those thoughts. Psychodynamic therapy explores unconscious patterns, but it may not provide the practical skills needed to regulate a nervous system that developed under chronic stress.

Adult children of PD parents need therapeutic approaches that address multiple levels simultaneously: the stored trauma in their bodies, the maladaptive patterns in their minds, the attachment wounds in their relationships, and the practical skills needed for daily emotional regulation.

Evidence-Based Approaches That Address PD Family Trauma

Research from BrightQuest Treatment Centers and other clinical sources shows that several therapeutic approaches are particularly effective for adults who grew up with personality-disordered parents. Each approach addresses different aspects of the healing process, and many people benefit from combining multiple modalities.

Dialectical Behavior Therapy Skills Training

Dialectical Behavior Therapy (DBT) was originally developed for people with Borderline Personality Disorder, but its skills training components are extraordinarily helpful for adult children of personality-disordered parents—regardless of which specific disorder their parent had.

DBT teaches four core skill sets that directly address the deficits created by PD family systems:

Distress Tolerance Skills These help you survive crisis situations without making them worse through impulsive actions. Children of PD parents often learned either to panic during crisis or to numb out completely. Distress tolerance provides a middle path.

Key skills include:

- TIPP (Temperature, Intense exercise, Paced breathing, Paired muscle relaxation)
- Radical acceptance of situations you can't change
- Self-soothing techniques that don't involve other people

- Distraction strategies for overwhelming emotions

Emotion Regulation Skills These help you understand, experience, and manage emotions effectively. Many PD families don't teach emotional literacy, leaving adult children confused about their internal experiences.

Key skills include:

- Identifying and naming emotions accurately
- Understanding the function emotions serve
- Reducing vulnerability to negative emotions
- Building positive emotional experiences
- Managing intense emotions without being overwhelmed

Interpersonal Effectiveness Skills These help you navigate relationships while maintaining self-respect and getting your needs met. PD families often teach either aggressive demand or passive submission, missing the middle ground of assertive communication.

Key skills include:

- Asking for what you need clearly and directly
- Saying no while maintaining relationships
- Managing conflict without sacrificing yourself or others
- Building and maintaining self-respect in interactions

Mindfulness Skills These help you stay present with your experience rather than being controlled by automatic reactions. Children of PD parents often live in constant anticipation of the next crisis, missing what's actually happening now.

Key skills include:

- Observing your thoughts and emotions without being controlled by them
- Describing experiences without interpretation or judgment
- Participating fully in present-moment activities

- Maintaining effectiveness rather than being "right"

Case Example: Maria's DBT Journey

Maria, 29, grew up with a borderline mother whose emotional crises dominated family life. She learned to manage Mom's emotions expertly but never learned to manage her own. By adulthood, Maria felt either completely numb or completely overwhelmed—there was no middle ground.

In DBT skills training, Maria learned that her emotional extremes made perfect sense given her childhood training. She'd learned to shut down her emotions to focus on Mom's needs, then feel overwhelmed when her suppressed feelings eventually surfaced.

The distress tolerance skills gave Maria tools for riding out emotional waves without either numbing out or being swept away. She learned to use cold water on her face to activate her mammalian dive response during panic attacks. She practiced radical acceptance for situations she couldn't control, like her mother's ongoing instability.

The emotion regulation skills helped Maria understand that her feelings had purpose and information, even when they felt overwhelming. She learned to identify emotions more specifically than "fine" or "terrible," and to take care of herself in ways that built resilience rather than requiring crisis management.

Most importantly, the interpersonal effectiveness skills taught Maria that she could maintain relationships without sacrificing herself. She learned to say no to her mother's emotional demands while still expressing care and concern. She discovered that boundaries could be loving rather than rejecting.

Eye Movement Desensitization and Reprocessing

EMDR was originally developed to treat PTSD from specific traumatic events, but adaptations have made it effective for complex relational trauma as well. EMDR helps process stored traumatic memories so they lose their emotional charge and stop interfering with current functioning.

For adult children of PD parents, EMDR can help with:

- Processing specific traumatic memories from childhood
- Reducing the emotional intensity of triggers
- Installing positive beliefs about self-worth and capability
- Integrating fragmented parts of the self

How EMDR Works for PD Family Trauma:

EMDR uses bilateral stimulation (usually eye movements) to help the brain process traumatic memories more completely. Many adult children of PD parents have memories that feel "stuck"—they can remember events but can't integrate the emotions, or they feel the emotions but can't access the memories clearly.

The process helps connect the logical, verbal parts of your brain with the emotional, somatic parts, allowing for more complete processing of difficult experiences.

Case Example: James's EMDR Experience

James, 35, grew up with a narcissistic father who turned every family interaction into a performance review. He could intellectually understand that his father's criticism came from Dad's own insecurity, but his body still responded to any form of evaluation as if he were facing a life-threatening attack.

Through EMDR, James was able to process specific memories of his father's criticism without being overwhelmed by the associated shame and terror. He worked through scenes like the time his father spent an hour criticizing his science fair project, pointing out every flaw while other parents celebrated their children's efforts.

As James processed these memories, the emotional charge began to diminish. He could remember his father's behavior without feeling like that scared eight-year-old boy. More importantly, he could receive feedback at work without his nervous system interpreting it as an attack on his fundamental worth.

Internal Family Systems Therapy

Internal Family Systems (IFS) recognizes that everyone has different "parts" within their personality—the achiever, the people-pleaser, the critic, the rebel. IFS helps you develop a healthy relationship with these internal parts rather than being controlled by them.

This approach is particularly helpful for adult children of PD parents because these family systems often create very developed "protector" parts that took over during childhood to manage impossible situations.

Key IFS Concepts:

- **Self**: The calm, curious, compassionate core of who you are
- **Exile parts**: Vulnerable parts that carry pain and were often hidden in PD families
- **Protector parts**: Parts that developed to manage threats and keep you safe
- **Firefighter parts**: Parts that emerge during crisis to handle emergencies

Case Example: Sarah's Parts Work

Sarah, 31, grew up with an OCPD father whose perfectionism created a household where mistakes felt catastrophic. She developed a strong "Manager" part that tried to anticipate and prevent any possible criticism, and a "Critic" part that constantly evaluated her performance.

These parts had served her well professionally—she was known for her attention to detail and high standards. But they were exhausting her and interfering with relationships because she couldn't relax or be spontaneous.

Through IFS work, Sarah learned to appreciate these parts while also helping them update their roles. Her Manager part didn't need to work overtime anymore because she wasn't living with her father's impossible standards. Her Critic part could focus on helping her improve rather than constantly finding fault.

Most importantly, Sarah began to access her Self—the part of her that was naturally curious, playful, and connected. This part had been buried under years of hypervigilance and perfectionism, but it was still there, waiting to reemerge.

Schema Therapy for Deep Pattern Change

Schema Therapy addresses the deep, unconscious patterns (schemas) that develop in childhood and continue to influence adult relationships and self-perception. These patterns often develop as adaptations to dysfunctional family environments.

Common schemas that develop in PD families include:

- **Abandonment/Instability**: Expecting that close relationships will end
- **Defectiveness/Shame**: Feeling fundamentally flawed or unworthy
- **Emotional Deprivation**: Expecting that emotional needs won't be met
- **Subjugation**: Automatically suppressing your needs to meet others'
- **Unrelenting Standards**: Believing you must be perfect to be acceptable

Schema Therapy helps identify these patterns, understand their origins, and gradually develop healthier alternatives through cognitive, emotional, and behavioral interventions.

Matching Therapy to Your PD Background

Different personality disorders in parents create different therapeutic needs in their adult children. Understanding your specific background helps you choose approaches most likely to address your particular adaptations.

Children of Cluster B Parents (Borderline, Narcissistic, Histrionic, Antisocial) often benefit most from:

- DBT for emotional regulation and relationship skills
- EMDR for processing traumatic memories of emotional chaos
- IFS for managing parts that developed to handle crisis and drama

Children of Cluster C Parents (Avoidant, Dependent, OCPD) often benefit most from:

- Schema Therapy for deep pattern change around perfectionism and self-worth
- IFS for accessing buried authentic parts
- DBT interpersonal skills for learning healthy assertiveness

Children of Cluster A Parents (Paranoid, Schizoid, Schizotypal) often benefit most from:

- Reality testing and cognitive approaches for updating inherited distortions
- Attachment-focused therapy for learning connection skills
- EMDR for processing neglect and emotional absence

Finding Qualified Therapists

Not all therapists are trained in trauma-informed approaches or understand the specific challenges faced by adult children of personality-disordered parents. Finding the right therapeutic match is essential for effective healing.

Questions to Ask Potential Therapists:

1. **What experience do you have working with adult children of parents with personality disorders?**
2. **Which therapeutic approaches do you use, and why do you think they'd be helpful for my situation?**
3. **How do you understand the difference between trauma responses and personality disorders?**
4. **What's your approach to helping clients who struggle with emotional regulation, boundaries, or relationships?**
5. **Do you have specific training in trauma-informed care?**

Red Flags to Watch For:

- Therapists who immediately want to diagnose you with a personality disorder
- Practitioners who minimize the impact of your childhood experiences
- Counselors who focus only on "positive thinking" without addressing underlying trauma
- Therapists who seem uncomfortable with emotional expression or family-of-origin work

Where to Find Qualified Therapists:

- Psychology Today's directory with trauma specialization filters
- EMDR International Association therapist locator
- DBT program directories
- Referrals from trauma-informed medical professionals
- Local mental health organizations with family trauma expertise

The Role of Medication

While therapy addresses the patterns and skills needed for healing, medication can sometimes provide support for the nervous system changes that resulted from growing up in chronic stress.

Adult children of PD parents often experience:

- **Anxiety disorders** from chronic hypervigilance

- **Depression** from emotional suppression and unmet developmental needs
- **ADHD-like symptoms** from difficulty focusing when constantly scanning for threats
- **Sleep disorders** from nervous systems that can't fully relax

Medication isn't a cure for trauma responses, but it can provide stability that makes therapeutic work more accessible. Some people find that addressing anxiety or depression with medication helps them engage more effectively in trauma-focused therapy.

Working with Psychiatrists:

If you consider medication, seek psychiatrists who understand trauma and can distinguish between trauma-based symptoms and other mental health conditions. Trauma responses often look like mood disorders or anxiety disorders but may require different treatment approaches.

Exercise: Therapy Readiness Assessment

This exercise helps you clarify your therapeutic goals and readiness for different types of healing work.

Current Symptoms Assessment: Rate how much each area currently interferes with your life (1 = not at all, 5 = severely):

- Emotional regulation (mood swings, numbness, overwhelm)
- Relationship difficulties (boundaries, intimacy, conflict)
- Anxiety and hypervigilance (constant worry, scanning for threats)
- Depression and hopelessness (emptiness, lack of meaning)
- Trauma responses (flashbacks, triggers, avoidance)
- Self-worth issues (shame, perfectionism, self-criticism)

Therapeutic Goals Clarification: What are your primary goals for therapy? Rank in order of importance:

- Learning to regulate emotions effectively

- Improving relationships and communication skills
- Processing traumatic memories from childhood
- Understanding family patterns and their current impact
- Developing authentic identity and self-worth
- Building practical life skills and confidence
- Creating meaning and purpose in life

Readiness Factors: Consider your current capacity for therapeutic work:

- Do you have adequate support systems for processing difficult material?
- Can you commit to regular therapy sessions for at least six months?
- Are you in a stable enough life situation to focus on internal work?
- Do you have coping skills for managing emotions between sessions?
- Are you willing to experience temporary increases in emotional intensity?

Your answers help identify which therapeutic approaches might be most beneficial and which preparatory work might be needed before starting intensive trauma therapy.

Integration and Hope

Lisa, whose story opened this chapter, eventually found healing through a combination of DBT skills training and EMDR processing. The DBT gave her practical tools for managing the emotional overwhelm that had characterized her adult life, while EMDR helped her process the stored memories of growing up with parents who couldn't see her as a separate person with her own needs.

The breakthrough came when Lisa realized that her childhood adaptations—the hypervigilance, the people-pleasing, the emotional suppression—weren't character flaws to be eliminated but survival strategies to be honored and updated. She could keep the empathy and attunement skills that served her well while learning to use them consciously rather than automatically.

Your healing journey will be unique to your specific experiences and current needs. The therapeutic approaches that work best for you may be different from what helps others, and you may need different approaches at different stages of your recovery.

Preparing for Deep Work

Understanding therapeutic options provides the foundation for the deeper healing work explored in the next chapter: reparenting. This approach recognizes that many adult children of PD parents missed crucial developmental experiences and need to consciously provide for themselves what their parents couldn't give them.

Reparenting isn't about becoming your own parent in a literal sense—it's about developing the internal nurturing, guidance, and support that healthy parenting provides, allowing you to heal developmental wounds and create the life you truly want.

Essential Learning Points

- **Evidence-based approaches** like DBT, EMDR, IFS, and Schema Therapy specifically address the complex trauma patterns created by personality-disordered parenting
- **DBT skills training** provides practical tools for emotional regulation, distress tolerance, interpersonal effectiveness, and mindfulness that directly address PD family deficits
- **EMDR processing** helps reduce the emotional charge of traumatic memories while IFS work helps develop healthy relationships with internal protective parts
- **Therapeutic matching** matters—different PD backgrounds create different healing needs requiring specific approaches and specialized therapist training
- **Qualified therapist selection** requires finding practitioners with trauma-informed training who understand the difference between trauma responses and personality disorders

- **Medication support** can provide nervous system stability that makes therapeutic work more accessible while addressing trauma-based anxiety and depression
- **Therapy readiness** involves assessing current symptoms, clarifying goals, and ensuring adequate support systems before beginning intensive trauma work

Chapter 11: The Reparenting Revolution

At thirty-five, Michael still heard his mother's voice every time he made a mistake. Not literally—she lived three states away—but the internal criticism was so automatic and harsh that friends often asked if someone was being mean to him. The voice would start the moment anything went wrong: "You're so careless. How could you be so stupid? You never think things through properly."

What Michael didn't realize was that this internal voice wasn't actually his mother anymore. It was a part of himself that had learned to anticipate her criticism as a way of trying to prevent it. The voice had once served as an early warning system, helping him avoid his OCPD mother's devastating evaluations by finding fault with himself first.

But now this internal critic was running his life, creating anxiety about decisions, paralysis around risk-taking, and constant dissatisfaction with his achievements. Michael needed to learn something that sounded strange but was revolutionizing trauma recovery: he needed to become a loving parent to himself.

Understanding Self-Reparenting

Self-reparenting is the process of consciously providing yourself with the emotional experiences, guidance, and support that healthy parenting should have given you. It's not about becoming childish or indulgent—it's about developing the internal nurturing and structure that allows for healthy adult functioning.

Research from Positive Psychology and attachment theory shows that many of the capacities we think of as innate—self-compassion, emotional regulation, internal motivation, healthy boundaries—actually develop through internalized parental functions. When these functions are missing or distorted, adults can consciously cultivate them through reparenting work.

The concept might feel foreign or even ridiculous at first. You might think, "I'm an adult. I shouldn't need parenting." But consider this: if you grew up in a family where emotional needs were ignored, criticism was constant, or love was conditional, you may never have internalized the supportive internal voice that most people take for granted.

What You Missed and Why It Matters

Healthy parenting provides several crucial functions that shape how we relate to ourselves and others throughout life:

Unconditional Positive Regard Healthy parents love their children simply for existing, not for what they achieve or how they behave. This creates an internal sense of inherent worth that remains stable despite external circumstances.

PD parents often provide conditional love based on performance, compliance, or meeting the parent's emotional needs. This creates adults who feel they must constantly earn their worth through achievement, people-pleasing, or perfection.

Emotional Attunement and Validation Healthy parents notice their children's emotional states, help them identify and name feelings, and provide comfort during distress. This teaches children that emotions are normal, manageable, and worthy of attention.

PD parents often can't provide consistent emotional attunement because their own emotional needs dominate the family system. Children learn that their feelings don't matter or are burdensome to others.

Healthy Boundaries and Limits Healthy parents set limits that protect children while also respecting their developing autonomy. They teach that boundaries are loving acts that protect relationships rather than walls that separate people.

PD parents often have poor boundaries themselves, either being overly intrusive or emotionally absent. Children don't learn to recognize their own needs and limits or to communicate them effectively.

Encouragement and Realistic Challenge Healthy parents encourage their children to try new things while providing support when challenges feel overwhelming. They help children develop confidence in their abilities while learning from mistakes.

PD parents often either demand perfection (creating fear of failure) or provide no structure or encouragement (creating lack of confidence in abilities).

Case Example: Rebecca's Reparenting Journey

Rebecca, 32, grew up with an avoidant mother who provided excellent practical care but no emotional warmth or connection. Mom's response to Rebecca's emotions was either to ignore them or to offer practical solutions without acknowledging the feelings involved.

As an adult, Rebecca functioned well professionally and maintained friendly relationships, but she felt empty and disconnected from herself. She didn't know how to comfort herself when upset, celebrate when something went well, or even identify what she was feeling beyond "fine" or "stressed."

Rebecca's reparenting work began with learning to check in with herself emotionally several times a day. She would pause and ask, "How am I feeling right now?" and "What do I need?" These questions felt silly at first because she'd never learned that her internal experience mattered.

She started practicing self-compassion by speaking to herself the way she would to a good friend facing the same situation. Instead of her automatic response of "Just deal with it," she learned to say things like, "This is really hard right now. It makes sense that you'd feel overwhelmed."

Rebecca also began creating comforting rituals for herself—making tea when she felt anxious, taking warm baths when she felt lonely, going for walks when she felt restless. These weren't luxuries or self-indulgence; they were the emotional care she'd never received as a child.

The breakthrough came when Rebecca realized she could provide for herself what her mother had never been able to give. She didn't need to wait for others to notice her needs or validate her feelings—she could offer herself the attention and care she craved.

Meeting Unmet Developmental Needs

Different developmental stages provide different crucial experiences. Reparenting involves identifying which developmental needs weren't met in your childhood and consciously providing those experiences for yourself now.

Infancy Needs: Safety and Unconditional Love If your infancy was disrupted by inconsistent caregiving, you might need to work on basic self-soothing and developing trust that your needs matter and will be met.

Reparenting practices:

- Creating safe, nurturing environments in your home
- Developing reliable self-care routines
- Learning to self-soothe without needing others
- Practicing positive self-talk about your inherent worth

Early Childhood Needs: Encouragement and Exploration If your early childhood was controlled or criticized, you might need to work on giving yourself permission to explore, play, and make mistakes without harsh judgment.

Reparenting practices:

- Encouraging yourself to try new things without demanding perfection
- Celebrating small wins and efforts, not just major achievements
- Allowing yourself to play and be silly without purpose
- Speaking to yourself with patience when you make mistakes

School Age Needs: Competence and Recognition If your school-age achievements were ignored or criticized, you might need to work on recognizing your own capabilities and celebrating your growth.

Reparenting practices:

- Acknowledging your efforts and improvements, not just final results
- Learning new skills for the joy of learning rather than for external approval
- Recognizing your unique strengths and talents
- Setting realistic challenges that build confidence

Adolescent Needs: Identity and Autonomy If your adolescent identity development was suppressed or controlled, you might need to work on discovering your authentic preferences and values.

Reparenting practices:

- Exploring your genuine interests without worrying about others' approval
- Making decisions based on your values rather than others' expectations
- Setting boundaries with family members who try to control your choices
- Expressing your authentic opinions and preferences

Case Example: David's Identity Recovery

David, 28, grew up with a narcissistic father who had detailed plans for David's life and couldn't tolerate any deviation from those expectations. David learned to suppress his own interests and preferences to maintain his father's approval.

As an adult, David was professionally successful in the career his father had chosen for him, but he felt like he was living someone else's life. He didn't know what he actually enjoyed, wanted, or valued because he'd never been allowed to explore these questions.

David's reparenting work involved giving himself permission to be curious about his authentic preferences. He started small—trying different types of food, music, and activities without judgment about what he "should" like.

He practiced asking himself questions his father had never asked: "What interests you about this? How does this make you feel? What would you choose if no one else's opinion mattered?"

David also worked on developing internal validation rather than seeking external approval for every decision. He learned to say, "I'm proud of myself for trying this" or "This choice feels right for me" instead of constantly seeking others' opinions about his choices.

The transformation happened gradually as David discovered he was actually quite different from the person his father had expected him to be. He was more creative, more collaborative, and more interested in helping others than in achieving status or wealth. These weren't defects to be corrected—they were authentic parts of himself that had been buried under years of performing for parental approval.

Cultivating Self-Compassion

Self-compassion is perhaps the most crucial aspect of reparenting work. It involves treating yourself with the same kindness you would offer a good friend facing similar struggles.

Research by Kristin Neff and others shows that self-compassion is more effective than self-criticism for motivation, learning, and emotional resilience. Yet many adult children of PD parents have developed harsh internal critics that constantly evaluate and find fault with their performance.

The Three Components of Self-Compassion:

Self-Kindness vs. Self-Criticism Instead of harsh judgment when you struggle or fail, self-kindness involves treating yourself with understanding and care. This doesn't mean excusing harmful behavior or avoiding responsibility—it means responding to mistakes with helpful guidance rather than attacking criticism.

Common Humanity vs. Isolation Instead of feeling like you're the only one who struggles or makes mistakes, common humanity recognizes that difficulty and imperfection are part of the shared human experience. Your struggles connect you to others rather than separating you.

Mindfulness vs. Over-Identification Instead of being overwhelmed by difficult emotions or completely suppressing them, mindfulness involves acknowledging your feelings without being controlled by them. You can observe your experience with curiosity rather than judgment.

Case Example: Lisa's Self-Compassion Development

Lisa, 30, grew up with an OCPD mother whose criticism was constant and detailed. Lisa internalized this critical voice so completely that she could barely make a decision without extensive self-attack about all the ways she might be wrong.

Lisa's self-compassion work began with simply noticing how harshly she spoke to herself. She started paying attention to her internal monologue and was shocked by how mean it was. She would never speak to another person the way she spoke to herself.

She began practicing what she called "the friend test"—asking herself, "Would I say this to a friend who was struggling with the same situation?" If the answer was no, she worked on finding a kinder way to address herself.

Lisa also worked on normalizing her struggles by recognizing that everyone faces challenges, makes mistakes, and has areas for growth. Her problems didn't make her uniquely flawed—they made her human.

The transformation was gradual but profound. Lisa's anxiety decreased as she stopped attacking herself for every perceived mistake. Her decision-making improved because she could consider options without fear of devastating self-criticism. Most importantly, she began to enjoy her life more because she wasn't constantly evaluating and finding fault with her experiences.

Building Internal Resources

Reparenting involves developing internal resources that can provide guidance, comfort, and support when external resources aren't available or reliable.

The Wise Adult Self This is the part of you that has perspective, compassion, and good judgment. It can offer guidance during difficult decisions and comfort during painful experiences. This wise self isn't perfect or all-knowing, but it cares about your wellbeing and wants you to thrive.

Developing your wise adult self involves:

- Regular reflection and journaling to access inner wisdom
- Meditation or mindfulness practices that create space for insight
- Asking yourself what guidance you would give to someone you love facing the same situation
- Trusting your intuition and internal knowing, even when others disagree

The Nurturing Parent Self This is the part of you that can provide comfort, encouragement, and care during difficult times. It offers the emotional support that healthy parents provide throughout life.

Developing your nurturing parent self involves:

- Learning to comfort yourself during distress with soothing words and actions
- Celebrating your achievements and efforts, not just final results
- Providing yourself with physical comfort through gentle touch, warm baths, cozy environments
- Speaking to yourself with the tone you would use with a beloved child

The Protective Parent Self This is the part of you that can set boundaries, advocate for your needs, and protect you from harmful situations or people. It provides the strength and clarity needed for healthy self-preservation.

Developing your protective parent self involves:

- Learning to recognize and communicate your needs and limits
- Setting boundaries with people who consistently disrespect or harm you
- Advocating for yourself in professional and personal situations
- Removing yourself from situations that are genuinely harmful to your wellbeing

Exercise: Inner Child Dialogue

This exercise helps you develop a conscious relationship with the younger parts of yourself that may still be carrying unmet needs or unprocessed pain.

Step 1: Create a Safe Space Find a quiet, private place where you won't be interrupted. You might want to have paper and pen available, or you can do this exercise entirely in your mind.

Step 2: Connect with Your Inner Child Close your eyes and imagine yourself as a child at an age when you felt particularly vulnerable or in need of support. This might be a specific age when trauma occurred, or simply a time when you felt alone or misunderstood.

Step 3: Initiate the Dialogue From your adult self, speak to your inner child with compassion and curiosity. You might start with:

- "Hi there. I see you, and I want to understand what you're feeling."
- "What do you need right now that you didn't get back then?"
- "How can I take better care of you now?"

Step 4: Listen to the Response Allow your inner child to respond without editing or judging what comes up. You might hear words, feel emotions, or sense physical sensations. Trust whatever emerges.

Step 5: Offer What's Needed Based on what your inner child communicates, offer what you can provide now. This might be:

- Validation: "What happened to you wasn't fair, and your feelings about it make complete sense."
- Protection: "I won't let anyone treat you that way anymore."
- Permission: "You're allowed to have needs and feelings, and they matter."
- Comfort: "I'm here with you now, and I'm not going anywhere."

Step 6: Make a Commitment End the dialogue by making a specific commitment about how you'll take better care of this younger part of yourself going forward.

Exercise: Self-Care Planning

This exercise helps you develop a personalized self-care plan based on your specific unmet developmental needs.

Identify Your Core Needs Review the developmental needs discussed earlier and identify which feel most relevant to your experience:

- Safety and unconditional love (infancy)
- Encouragement and exploration (early childhood)
- Competence and recognition (school age)
- Identity and autonomy (adolescence)

Create Specific Practices For each identified need, create 2-3 specific practices you can use to meet that need for yourself:

For Safety and Unconditional Love:

- Daily affirmations about your inherent worth
- Creating a cozy, nurturing environment in your home
- Developing consistent self-care routines

For Encouragement and Exploration:

- Trying one new thing each week without pressure to excel
- Celebrating efforts and improvements, not just achievements
- Giving yourself permission to play and be creative

For Competence and Recognition:

- Keeping a log of your daily accomplishments, including small ones
- Learning new skills for the joy of learning
- Acknowledging your unique strengths and talents

For Identity and Autonomy:

- Regular check-ins with yourself about your authentic preferences
- Making decisions based on your values rather than others' expectations
- Expressing your genuine opinions and interests

Schedule Your Practices Self-care isn't selfish—it's necessary maintenance for healthy adult functioning. Schedule your reparenting practices like you would any other important appointment with yourself.

The Transformation Process

Reparenting work creates profound changes that often surprise people with their power and reach. As you begin to provide yourself with missing developmental experiences, several shifts typically occur:

Increased Self-Trust As you practice listening to your needs and providing appropriate care, you develop confidence in your ability to handle life's challenges. You stop looking to others to rescue you or tell you what to do because you trust your own judgment and capability.

Improved Relationships Paradoxically, as you become better at meeting your own needs, your relationships with others improve. You're no longer desperately seeking from others what you can provide for yourself, which allows for more balanced, reciprocal connections.

Reduced Anxiety and Depression Many symptoms that seemed like mental illness actually represent unmet developmental needs. As those needs are addressed through reparenting work, anxiety and depression often significantly improve.

Enhanced Creativity and Authenticity When you're no longer spending energy trying to earn love or avoid criticism, that energy becomes available for authentic self-expression and creative pursuits.

Preparing for Boundaries

Michael, whose story opened this chapter, gradually learned to replace his mother's harsh internal voice with a compassionate inner parent who could offer guidance without attack. He didn't eliminate his capacity for self-reflection or improvement—he learned to pursue growth from love rather than from fear of criticism.

Your reparenting work provides the foundation for the next crucial aspect of recovery: boundaries. When you've learned to meet your own needs and treat yourself with compassion, you're ready to set limits that protect your wellbeing while maintaining healthy relationships with others.

The Journey Continues

Reparenting isn't a destination but an ongoing practice of conscious self-care and emotional development. As you continue to grow and face new challenges, you'll discover new ways to support yourself and meet needs that may have been buried for decades.

The next chapter explores how to set and maintain boundaries—the protective limits that allow you to have relationships without sacrificing yourself in the process.

Core Transformations

- **Self-reparenting** involves consciously providing yourself with the emotional experiences, guidance, and support that healthy parenting should have given you during development
- **Unmet developmental needs** from infancy through adolescence can be addressed in adulthood through targeted reparenting practices specific to each stage's requirements
- **Self-compassion** replaces harsh internal criticism with the same kindness you'd offer a good friend, creating internal support rather than constant self-attack
- **Internal resources** like wise adult self, nurturing parent self, and protective parent self can be developed to provide ongoing guidance, comfort, and protection
- **Inner child dialogue** creates conscious connection with younger parts that still carry unmet needs, allowing for healing conversation and commitment

- **Systematic self-care planning** addresses specific developmental gaps through regular practices that meet your unique combination of unmet needs
- **Reparenting transformation** increases self-trust, improves relationships, reduces anxiety and depression, and enhances authentic self-expression through meeting your own emotional needs

Chapter 12: Boundaries - The Foundation of Recovery

The text message seemed innocent enough: "Haven't heard from you in a while. Hope everything's okay. Call me soon!" But Jennifer's stomach clenched when she saw her mother's name on the screen. It had been three weeks since their last conversation—three peaceful weeks without emotional crisis management, guilt trips, or having to manage her mother's feelings about Jennifer's adult life choices.

Jennifer knew what "Call me soon" really meant. It meant her mother was feeling abandoned and would spend the next conversation cataloging all the ways Jennifer was failing as a daughter. It meant at least an hour of emotional labor to restore her mother's sense of security. It meant choosing between her own peace of mind and her mother's emotional needs.

At thirty-one, Jennifer still felt guilty for wanting space from her borderline mother's intensity. She knew intellectually that she had the right to boundaries, but emotionally it felt like abandonment, rejection, and cruelty. This internal conflict—between knowing what she needed and feeling terrible about needing it—captures the core boundary challenge for adult children of personality-disordered parents.

Why Boundaries Feel Impossible

Boundaries are limits that protect your emotional, physical, and mental wellbeing while allowing you to maintain relationships with others. They're not walls that shut people out—they're gates that let healthy connection in while keeping harmful behavior out.

For most people, boundaries develop naturally through childhood experiences of having their "no" respected, their privacy protected, and their individual needs acknowledged. But children of personality-disordered parents often learn the opposite lessons:

- Your needs don't matter as much as others' feelings

- Saying "no" causes devastating pain to people you love
- Taking care of yourself is selfish and harmful to relationships
- Love requires sacrificing your comfort for others' comfort
- You're responsible for managing other people's emotional reactions

These lessons create adults who feel guilty for having needs, apologize for taking up space, and experience physical anxiety when they have to set limits with others.

The Boundary Myths That Keep You Trapped

Several myths about boundaries prevent adult children of PD parents from developing healthy limits:

Myth 1: Boundaries are mean or selfish Healthy boundaries are actually loving because they prevent resentment and allow for genuine connection. When you constantly sacrifice your needs, you eventually become resentful, withdrawn, or explosive—none of which helps your relationships.

Myth 2: Other people's feelings are more important than your wellbeing Your emotional and physical wellbeing matters just as much as anyone else's. You can care about others' feelings without being responsible for managing them or sacrificing your own needs to prevent their discomfort.

Myth 3: Good people don't have boundaries Good people absolutely have boundaries. Boundary-free people often enable others' harmful behavior, become martyrs who create guilt in others, or burn out from giving more than they have to give.

Myth 4: Boundaries will destroy your relationships Healthy relationships become stronger with clear boundaries. Unhealthy relationships may end when boundaries are introduced, but this reveals that the relationship was based on your willingness to be exploited rather than genuine mutual care.

Internal vs. External Boundaries

Most people think of boundaries as external limits—what you will and won't allow others to do. But for adult children of PD parents, internal boundaries are often more challenging and equally important.

Internal Boundaries These are the limits you set with yourself about what you will and won't think about, feel responsible for, or allow to control your emotional state.

Examples of internal boundaries:

- Not taking responsibility for others' emotional reactions to your choices
- Refusing to ruminate endlessly about whether you've hurt someone's feelings
- Not allowing your parent's mood to determine your mood
- Setting limits on how much time you'll spend worrying about others' problems
- Not allowing guilt to override your judgment about what's healthy

External Boundaries These are the limits you communicate to others about what you will and won't accept in terms of behavior, communication, and demands on your time and energy.

Examples of external boundaries:

- Not answering phone calls after 9 PM or before 8 AM
- Refusing to discuss certain topics that consistently lead to conflict
- Limiting visits or contact to amounts that don't exhaust you
- Not lending money to family members who don't repay debts
- Ending conversations that become abusive or manipulative

Case Example: Maria's Boundary Development

Maria, 29, grew up with a narcissistic mother who treated her like a confidante and emotional support system rather than a daughter. Mom would call several times a week to discuss her problems, complain about other people, and seek validation for her decisions.

As an adult, Maria dreaded these calls but felt guilty for not being more available. She tried setting external boundaries by screening calls or limiting conversation time, but she'd spend hours afterward worrying about whether she'd been cruel or selfish.

Maria realized she needed internal boundaries before external ones would work. She started by refusing to take responsibility for her mother's emotional reactions to her limits. When Mom got upset about a shortened phone call, Maria practiced thinking, "Mom's feelings about my boundaries are her responsibility to manage."

She also set internal limits on guilt. Instead of spending hours analyzing whether she'd been a bad daughter, Maria gave herself a ten-minute limit for processing these concerns, then consciously redirected her attention to her own life and relationships.

The external boundaries became easier once the internal ones were in place. Maria could limit phone calls to thirty minutes because she wasn't spending two hours afterward managing guilt and anxiety about her mother's reaction.

PD-Specific Boundary Challenges

Different personality disorders create different boundary challenges for their adult children:

Borderline Parents and Abandonment Boundaries Children of borderline parents often struggle with boundaries because any limit feels like abandonment to the parent, triggering intense emotional reactions that the child learned to prevent at all costs.

Necessary boundaries:

- Not being responsible for preventing your parent's emotional crises
- Maintaining relationships and activities your parent sees as threatening
- Refusing to be the primary source of emotional support
- Not apologizing for having your own life and relationships

Narcissistic Parents and Performance Boundaries Children of narcissistic parents often struggle with boundaries around achievement, image, and independence because the parent views the child's choices as reflections of their own worth.

Necessary boundaries:

- Making life choices based on your values rather than your parent's image
- Not performing success or happiness to maintain parental approval
- Refusing to be criticized or controlled for being different from parental expectations
- Not accepting responsibility for your parent's disappointment in your choices

OCPD Parents and Perfectionism Boundaries Children of OCPD parents often struggle with boundaries around standards, control, and decision-making because the parent believes their way is the only correct way.

Necessary boundaries:

- Making decisions using your own judgment rather than seeking parental approval
- Not accepting criticism for doing things differently than the parent would
- Refusing to defend your choices to someone who won't accept your autonomy
- Not allowing your parent's anxiety about your methods to change your approach

Case Example: Tom's Narcissistic Father Boundaries

Tom, 33, grew up with a narcissistic father who had detailed expectations for Tom's career, relationships, and lifestyle. Dad couldn't tolerate Tom making choices that didn't align with his vision of success and would launch into lectures about Tom's "potential" whenever Tom pursued his own interests.

When Tom decided to become a teacher instead of pursuing business, his father's reaction was devastating. "You're throwing your life away. You're smarter than this. I'm disappointed in the man you're becoming." The criticism felt like a complete rejection of Tom's worth as a person.

Tom's boundary work involved recognizing that his father's disappointment was about Dad's ego, not about Tom's actual wellbeing or happiness. Tom learned to respond to criticism by saying, "I understand you have different preferences for my life, but I'm comfortable with my choices."

The real breakthrough came when Tom stopped trying to convince his father that his choices were valid. He realized that his father wasn't interested in understanding Tom's perspective—he wanted Tom to conform to his expectations. Once Tom accepted this, he could maintain the relationship without sacrificing his autonomy.

Tom set clear boundaries: he wouldn't discuss career decisions with his father, wouldn't defend his life choices, and would end conversations that became critical lectures. His father initially escalated his criticism, but eventually accepted that Tom wouldn't engage with these topics.

Managing Guilt and Resistance

The most challenging aspect of boundary setting for adult children of PD parents is managing the intense guilt that arises when they start prioritizing their own wellbeing.

This guilt often feels overwhelming because it connects to childhood messages that your needs hurt others and that love requires self-sacrifice. The guilt feels like evidence that you're being selfish or cruel, when actually it's evidence that you're updating patterns that no longer serve you.

Strategies for Managing Boundary Guilt:

Normalize the guilt without letting it control your decisions Recognize that feeling guilty about boundaries is normal given your upbringing, but don't use the guilt as evidence that your boundaries are wrong.

Focus on long-term relationship health rather than short-term comfort Boundaries may cause temporary discomfort for others, but they prevent the long-term resentment and disconnection that comes from one-sided relationships.

Remember that others' emotional reactions belong to them You can care about someone's feelings without being responsible for managing those feelings or changing your behavior to prevent their discomfort.

Practice self-compassion about the adjustment period Both you and others need time to adjust to new boundaries. Be patient with the process rather than expecting immediate acceptance.

Case Example: Linda's Dependent Mother Boundaries

Linda, 35, grew up with a dependent mother who relied on Linda for emotional support, decision-making help, and constant reassurance. Mom would call several times a day asking for advice about minor decisions and become anxious if Linda didn't immediately respond to texts.

Linda felt trapped between her mother's needs and her own desire for independence. She wanted to help but felt overwhelmed by the constant demands for attention and guidance.

Linda's boundary work involved teaching her mother to handle minor decisions independently. Instead of immediately providing advice, Linda started saying, "What do you think you should do?" or "What are your options?"

She also limited her availability for non-emergency calls to specific times of day and stopped responding immediately to texts that weren't urgent. Her mother's anxiety increased initially, but she gradually developed more confidence in her own decision-making abilities.

The guilt was intense at first. Linda felt like she was abandoning her mother when she didn't provide immediate support. But she realized that her constant availability had actually prevented her mother from developing independence. The boundaries were ultimately more loving than the enabling had been.

Boundary Scripts for Common Situations

Having prepared responses for common boundary violations helps you respond consistently rather than getting caught off-guard and reverting to old patterns.

For Emotional Manipulation: "I can see you're upset, but I'm not going to change my decision based on your emotional reaction."

For Guilt Trips: "I understand you're disappointed, but I'm comfortable with my choice."

For Criticism of Your Boundaries: "I know my boundaries might feel uncomfortable, but they're necessary for me to maintain a healthy relationship with you."

For Demands for Justification: "I've made my decision, and I don't need to defend it."

For Emergency Calls About Non-Emergencies: "This doesn't sound like an emergency. Let's talk during our regular call time."

For Refusal to Accept Your Limits: "I've explained my boundary clearly. Continuing to argue about it won't change my position."

Exercise: Boundary Assessment

This exercise helps you identify areas where boundaries are needed and assess your current boundary skills.

Rate each area from 1 (no boundaries) to 5 (healthy boundaries):

Time and Availability:

- Can you say no to requests that would overextend you?
- Do you maintain limits on when you're available for calls/texts?
- Are you able to prioritize your own schedule and commitments?

Emotional Responsibility:

- Can you avoid taking responsibility for others' emotional reactions?
- Are you able to maintain your own emotional state when others are upset?
- Do you recognize the difference between empathy and emotional caretaking?

Decision Making:

- Can you make choices based on your own values and preferences?
- Are you able to resist pressure to change decisions others don't like?
- Do you feel confident in your judgment without constant external validation?

Physical Boundaries:

- Can you ask for space when you need it?
- Are you comfortable with appropriate levels of physical affection?
- Do you feel ownership of your personal space and belongings?

Communication Boundaries:

- Can you refuse to engage in conversations that consistently become hostile?
- Are you able to express disagreement without becoming defensive?
- Do you feel comfortable ending conversations that violate your boundaries?

Areas with scores of 1-2 indicate boundary development opportunities. Areas with scores of 4-5 indicate existing strengths you can build upon.

Exercise: Boundary Practice Scenarios

Practice responses to common boundary challenges in low-risk situations before using them in high-stakes family interactions.

Scenario 1: The Guilt Trip Someone says: "I guess you're too busy for family now." Practice responses:

- "I care about you, and I also need to maintain balance in my life."
- "My schedule doesn't reflect how much I care about you."
- "I understand you miss me. Let's find a time that works for both of us."

Scenario 2: The Criticism Someone says: "You've really changed, and not for the better." Practice responses:

- "Change is part of growth. I'm sorry you're uncomfortable with it."
- "I'm becoming more honest about my needs. That's healthy."

- "We might see this differently, and that's okay."

Scenario 3: The Emergency Someone calls with a non-urgent problem demanding immediate attention. Practice responses:

- "This sounds important but not urgent. Let's talk tomorrow."
- "I'm not available right now, but I can call you back at [specific time]."
- "What have you already tried to solve this problem?"

Scenario 4: The Manipulation Someone says: "If you really loved me, you would..." Practice responses:

- "My love for you isn't measured by my willingness to do what you want."
- "I can love you and still have different boundaries."
- "Love and boundaries can coexist."

Practice these responses until they feel natural rather than rehearsed. The goal is having healthy responses available when you need them rather than being caught off-guard by manipulation or guilt.

The Paradox of Healthy Boundaries

One of the most surprising discoveries people make when they start setting boundaries is that their relationships often improve rather than deteriorate. Healthy people respect boundaries and appreciate knowing where they stand. Unhealthy people may resist boundaries initially but often adjust when they realize the limits are consistent and non-negotiable.

The relationships that end due to boundaries usually weren't healthy relationships to begin with—they were based on your willingness to sacrifice your wellbeing rather than on mutual care and respect.

Jennifer, whose story opened this chapter, eventually learned to respond to her mother's guilt-inducing texts with simple, caring responses that didn't sacrifice her own peace: "I love you, and I'll call you this weekend." She stopped feeling responsible for her mother's emotional reactions to her normal adult need for space.

The relationship actually improved because Jennifer was no longer resentful about constant emotional labor. When she did engage with her mother, she could be genuinely present rather than mentally calculating how quickly she could escape.

Building Your Boundary Foundation

Boundaries aren't just about saying no—they're about creating the conditions that allow yes to be meaningful. When you protect your time, energy, and emotional wellbeing through appropriate limits, you have more to offer in your relationships.

The next chapter explores practical emotional regulation skills that support your boundary development and help you manage the intense emotions that can arise during recovery work.

Boundary Essentials

- **Boundaries protect wellbeing** while maintaining relationships, serving as gates that allow healthy connection while keeping harmful behavior out
- **Internal boundaries** involve limits on what you'll feel responsible for or allow to control your emotional state, often more challenging than external limits
- **PD-specific challenges** require different boundary approaches—borderline parents trigger abandonment fears, narcissistic parents challenge performance expectations, OCPD parents resist autonomy
- **Guilt management** requires recognizing that boundary guilt is normal given your upbringing without using guilt as evidence that boundaries are wrong
- **Prepared responses** for common manipulation tactics help maintain consistent boundaries rather than reverting to old patterns when caught off-guard

- **Boundary assessment** identifies areas needing development and builds on existing strengths rather than trying to change everything simultaneously
- **Healthy relationships improve** with clear boundaries while unhealthy relationships may end, revealing they were based on exploitation rather than mutual care

Chapter 13: Emotional Regulation Toolkit

The panic attack hit Sarah in the middle of a team meeting. Her manager had asked a simple question about project timelines, but something in his tone triggered her childhood alarm system. Suddenly she was eight years old again, trying to explain to her obsessive-compulsive father why her homework wasn't perfect, bracing for the detailed criticism that would follow.

Her heart raced, her breathing became shallow, and her thoughts spiraled into catastrophic predictions about being fired, humiliated, and proving once again that she wasn't competent enough to succeed. The rational part of her mind knew this response was out of proportion to the situation, but knowing it didn't make it stop.

This is emotional dysregulation—the nervous system's automatic response to perceived threats, even when those threats exist only in memory or imagination. For adult children of personality-disordered parents, emotional regulation often feels like trying to control a fire alarm that goes off every time someone toasts bread.

Understanding Your Inherited Nervous System

Growing up with personality-disordered parents doesn't just create psychological patterns—it creates neurobiological adaptations that affect how your nervous system processes and responds to everyday situations.

Research shows that chronic childhood stress alters the development of brain regions responsible for emotional regulation, threat assessment, and decision-making. Your nervous system learned to prioritize survival over connection, vigilance over relaxation, and crisis management over steady functioning.

These adaptations served you well in a chaotic family environment, but they can create problems in adult situations that don't require constant alertness or crisis respons

The Three-Brain Model of Trauma Response

Understanding how your brain responds to stress helps you work with your nervous system rather than fighting against it. The triune brain model explains three levels of brain function that can become dysregulated in adult children of PD parents:

The Reptilian Brain (Brain Stem) This is your survival brain—responsible for basic functions like breathing, heart rate, and fight-or-flight responses. When this system is activated, you feel physically threatened even when the danger is emotional or imaginary.

Signs of reptilian brain activation:

- Racing heart, shallow breathing, muscle tension
- Tunnel vision or difficulty concentrating
- Feeling like you need to escape or fight
- Physical sensations of danger without clear external threats

The Mammalian Brain (Limbic System) This is your emotional brain—responsible for attachment, memory, and emotional responses. When this system is overwhelmed, you may feel flooded by emotions or completely numb.

Signs of mammalian brain overwhelm:

- Emotional reactions that feel too big for the situation
- Flashbacks to childhood experiences
- Feeling emotionally flooded or completely shut down
- Difficulty accessing logical thinking

The Human Brain (Neocortex) This is your thinking brain—responsible for planning, analysis, and conscious decision-making. When the lower brain systems are activated, this higher brain often goes "offline," making rational thought and problem-solving difficult.

Signs of neocortex disconnection:

- Difficulty making decisions or thinking clearly
- Forgetting important information or skills you normally have
- Feeling "stupid" or incompetent in ways that don't match your actual abilities
- Unable to access solutions that would normally seem obvious

DBT Skills by PD Background Type

Dialectical Behavior Therapy offers practical tools for emotional regulation that can be adapted based on your specific childhood experiences with different personality disorders.

For Children of Cluster B Parents (Dramatic/Emotional) Growing up with borderline, narcissistic, histrionic, or antisocial parents often creates adults who struggle with emotional intensity and relationship chaos.

Primary DBT skills needed:

- **Distress tolerance** for managing emotional storms without making them worse
- **Interpersonal effectiveness** for maintaining relationships without drama or manipulation
- **Emotion regulation** for experiencing feelings without being overwhelmed

For Children of Cluster C Parents (Anxious/Fearful) Growing up with avoidant, dependent, or OCPD parents often creates adults who struggle with perfectionism, anxiety, and emotional suppression.

Primary DBT skills needed:

- **Mindfulness** for staying present instead of worrying about future problems
- **Distress tolerance** for accepting "good enough" instead of demanding perfection
- **Emotion regulation** for accessing and expressing feelings that were suppressed

For Children of Cluster A Parents (Odd/Eccentric) Growing up with paranoid, schizoid, or schizotypal parents often creates adults who struggle with social connection and reality testing.

Primary DBT skills needed:

- **Interpersonal effectiveness** for building and maintaining social connections
- **Mindfulness** for staying grounded in present reality
- **Emotion regulation** for understanding and expressing emotions appropriately

Case Example: Marcus's Emotional Regulation Journey

Marcus, 32, grew up with a borderline mother whose emotional crises dominated family life. He learned to suppress his own emotions to focus on managing Mom's feelings, but this left him unable to understand or regulate his own emotional experiences.

As an adult, Marcus felt either completely numb or completely overwhelmed. He could handle others' emotional crises brilliantly but had no idea how to manage his own feelings when they arose.

Marcus began learning DBT skills starting with basic emotion identification. He practiced naming emotions more specifically than "fine" or "terrible"—learning to distinguish between frustrated and angry, disappointed and sad, worried and terrified.

He learned that emotions had important information to offer. His anger told him that someone had crossed a boundary. His sadness indicated that he'd lost something important. His fear warned him about potential threats. Instead of suppressing these signals, he learned to listen to them and respond appropriately.

The breakthrough came when Marcus learned to self-soothe during emotional storms instead of either exploding or shutting down. He practiced techniques like cold water on his face to activate his mammalian dive response, bilateral stimulation through rhythmic movement, and grounding techniques that connected him to his physical environment.

Mindfulness and Grounding Techniques

Mindfulness for trauma survivors isn't about emptying your mind or achieving perfect peace—it's about developing the ability to observe your experience without being controlled by it.

The STOP Technique When you notice emotional overwhelm beginning:

- **S**top what you're doing
- **T**ake a breath
- **O**bserve what's happening in your body, emotions, and thoughts
- **P**roceed with conscious choice rather than automatic reaction

5-4-3-2-1 Grounding This technique helps bring your nervous system back to the present moment:

- Name **5 things** you can see
- Name **4 things** you can touch
- Name **3 things** you can hear
- Name **2 things** you can smell
- Name **1 thing** you can taste

Bilateral Stimulation This activates both sides of your brain and nervous system, promoting integration and calm:

- Cross-lateral movements like marching in place while touching opposite hand to knee
- Butterfly hugs—wrapping arms around yourself and alternately patting each shoulder
- Eye movements—slowly looking left and right while keeping head still

Case Example: Jennifer's Mindfulness Practice

Jennifer, 30, grew up with a histrionic mother whose dramatic emotional displays taught Jennifer that normal feelings weren't intense enough to be valid. Jennifer learned to escalate her emotions to get attention, but this left her exhausted by constant emotional intensity.

Jennifer's mindfulness practice began with learning to notice emotions before they became overwhelming. She practiced the STOP technique throughout the day, pausing to check in with her internal experience before it reached crisis levels.

She discovered that her emotions actually had a natural ebb and flow when she didn't amplify them for dramatic effect. Sadness would arise, peak, and naturally decrease if she just let it exist without performance. Anger would provide information and then dissipate if she listened to its message without creating a production around it.

The most profound change was learning to tolerate ordinary emotional states—contentment, mild satisfaction, quiet joy—without feeling like she needed to intensify them to make them "real."

Flashback Management

Emotional flashbacks occur when current situations trigger stored memories and emotions from childhood, causing you to react as if past danger is present now. Unlike visual flashbacks, emotional flashbacks may not include clear memories—just overwhelming feelings that seem disproportionate to current circumstances.

Recognizing Emotional Flashbacks:

- Feeling suddenly overwhelmed by shame, fear, anger, or despair
- Reactions that feel too big for the current situation
- Feeling like a younger version of yourself
- Physical sensations of danger without clear external threats
- Thoughts that seem to come from childhood rather than current reality

The Flashback Management Protocol:

1. **Recognize the flashback**: "This feels like the past, not the present"
2. **Orient to current reality**: Look around, name where you are, what year it is, how old you are now
3. **Breathe and ground**: Use physical techniques to calm your nervous system
4. **Reassure the triggered part**: "You're safe now. That was then, this is now. I'm here with you"
5. **Identify the trigger**: What current situation activated this childhood response?
6. **Choose a conscious response**: How do you want to handle the current situation based on your adult resources?

Case Example: David's Flashback Recovery

David, 31, grew up with an antisocial father who used manipulation and emotional exploitation as normal interaction styles. David learned to constantly assess others' motives and protect himself from being used.

As an adult, David experienced emotional flashbacks whenever he felt someone might be trying to manipulate or exploit him. A friend asking for a favor could trigger overwhelming suspicion and rage that belonged to childhood experiences with his father.

David learned to recognize these flashbacks by their intensity and the paranoid quality of his thoughts. When he felt that familiar combination of rage and suspicion, he would pause and ask himself, "Is this about now or then?"

He developed a practice of grounding himself in current reality by looking around his environment and reminding himself of his adult resources: "I'm 31 years old. I have good judgment about people. I can say no if I want to. I have many genuine friends who care about me."

This didn't eliminate David's appropriate caution about exploitation—his childhood had taught him useful skills for recognizing manipulation. But it allowed him to respond to current situations based on current information rather than being controlled by childhood fears.

Distress Tolerance Building

Distress tolerance involves your ability to survive difficult emotions and situations without making them worse through impulsive or destructive actions. Many adult children of PD parents never learned that difficult emotions are temporary and survivable.

The TIPP Technique TIPP rapidly changes your body chemistry to reduce emotional intensity:

Temperature - Use cold water on your face, hold ice cubes, or take a cold shower to activate your mammalian dive response, which automatically slows your heart rate and calms your nervous system.

Intense Exercise - Do jumping jacks, run in place, or do pushups for several minutes to burn off stress chemicals and reset your nervous system.

Paced Breathing - Breathe in for 4 counts, hold for 4, exhale for 6. Making your exhale longer than your inhale activates your parasympathetic nervous system.

Paired Muscle Relaxation - Tense all your muscles for 5 seconds, then release completely. This helps discharge physical tension and promotes relaxation.

Radical Acceptance This skill helps you stop fighting reality when you can't change what's happening. Radical acceptance doesn't mean you like what's happening or that you're giving up on change—it means you're accepting the current reality so you can respond effectively rather than wasting energy fighting what already is.

Steps to radical acceptance:

1. Notice when you're fighting reality ("This shouldn't be happening")
2. Remind yourself that fighting reality creates additional suffering
3. Practice accepting statements: "This is what's happening right now"
4. Focus your energy on what you can control rather than what you can't

Self-Soothing Techniques Develop a toolkit of activities that comfort you without requiring other people or potentially harmful substances:

- Physical: warm baths, soft textures, comfortable positions, gentle movement
- Visual: beautiful images, calming colors, nature scenes, art
- Auditory: soothing music, nature sounds, calming voices
- Olfactory: pleasant scents, essential oils, favorite foods cooking
- Gustatory: comforting foods, warm drinks, favorite flavors

Case Example: Lisa's Distress Tolerance Development

Lisa, 28, grew up with an OCPD mother whose perfectionism made any mistake feel catastrophic. Lisa learned to avoid anything she might not do perfectly, which severely limited her life experiences and opportunities.

Lisa's distress tolerance work began with deliberately practicing "good enough" in low-stakes situations. She would send emails without proofreading them multiple times, submit work that was complete but not perfect, and make decisions without researching every possible option.

When the anxiety and shame arose from these imperfect actions, Lisa used TIPP techniques to manage the distress. Cold water on her face helped calm her immediate panic. Intense exercise burned off the stress chemicals that made her want to fix or improve everything. Paced breathing helped her nervous system settle.

Most importantly, Lisa practiced radical acceptance of imperfection. Instead of fighting the reality that she'd made a mistake or done something less than perfectly, she practiced saying, "This is good enough for now" and "Mistakes are part of learning."

Over time, Lisa discovered that most of her "imperfect" work was actually quite good, and that the anxiety she'd experienced about imperfection was much worse than the actual consequences of being less than perfect.

Exercise: TIPP Practice

This exercise helps you build familiarity with TIPP techniques so they're available when you need them most.

Temperature Practice:

- Fill a bowl with cold water (50-60 degrees)
- Hold your breath and put your face in the water from temples to chin for 30 seconds
- Alternative: Hold ice cubes in your hands or place a cold pack on your eyes and cheeks
- Notice how this affects your heart rate and overall arousal level

Intense Exercise Practice:

- Do jumping jacks for 60 seconds
- Alternative: run in place, do pushups, or any vigorous movement
- Notice the shift in your emotional state before and after
- Practice this when you're not in crisis so it's familiar when needed

Paced Breathing Practice:

- Breathe in for 4 counts through your nose
- Hold for 4 counts
- Exhale for 6 counts through your mouth

- Repeat for 2-3 minutes
- Notice the calming effect on your nervous system

Paired Muscle Relaxation Practice:

- Tense all muscles in your body as tightly as possible for 5 seconds
- Release suddenly and completely
- Notice the contrast between tension and relaxation
- Repeat 2-3 times, paying attention to the release of physical stress

Exercise: Emotion Diary

This exercise helps you develop emotional awareness and identify patterns in your emotional responses.

Daily Tracking: For one week, note three times each day:

Morning Check-in:

- What am I feeling right now?
- What's my energy level?
- What am I anticipating about today?

Midday Check-in:

- How have my emotions shifted since morning?
- What situations have affected my mood?
- What do I need right now to feel balanced?

Evening Check-in:

- What emotions did I experience today?
- Which situations triggered strong reactions?
- How did I handle challenging emotions?
- What did I learn about my emotional patterns?

Weekly Pattern Analysis: Look for patterns across the week:

- Which emotions came up most frequently?
- What situations consistently triggered strong reactions?
- Which coping strategies were most helpful?
- What emotional needs aren't being met regularly?

Use this information to identify your emotional triggers, effective coping strategies, and areas where additional support might be helpful.

Building Your Regulation Toolkit

Emotional regulation isn't about controlling or suppressing your emotions—it's about developing a healthy relationship with your emotional experience so feelings can provide information and motivation without overwhelming your capacity to think and choose consciously.

Your emotional regulation toolkit should include techniques for different types of situations:

- **Crisis management** tools for emotional emergencies
- **Daily maintenance** practices for ongoing emotional health
- **Trigger management** strategies for predictable difficult situations
- **Self-soothing** techniques for comfort during distress
- **Grounding** practices for staying present and connected

Sarah, whose story opened this chapter, eventually learned to recognize the early warning signs of her anxiety spiral and interrupt it before it became overwhelming. She couldn't eliminate all emotional reactions to stressful situations, but she could choose how to respond to those reactions.

The goal isn't emotional perfection—it's emotional flexibility and choice.

Preparing for Relationship Healing

Your emotional regulation skills provide the foundation for the relationship recovery work explored in the next chapter. When you can manage your own emotional responses consciously, you're better equipped to break generational patterns and build the secure, healthy relationships you want.

Understanding and regulating your emotions is the bridge between understanding your past and creating your future.

Regulation Mastery Points

- **Emotional dysregulation** results from neurobiological adaptations to chronic childhood stress, creating nervous system responses designed for survival rather than thriving
- **Three-brain understanding** helps recognize when reptilian survival responses, mammalian emotional flooding, or neocortex shutdown is occurring during stress
- **DBT skills adaptation** varies by PD background—Cluster B survivors need intensity management, Cluster C survivors need anxiety and perfectionism tools, Cluster A survivors need connection and reality-testing skills
- **Mindfulness practices** like STOP technique and 5-4-3-2-1 grounding help observe experience without being controlled by automatic reactions
- **Flashback management** involves recognizing when current triggers activate childhood responses and consciously orienting to present reality and adult resources
- **Distress tolerance skills** including TIPP technique and radical acceptance help survive difficult emotions without impulsive actions that worsen situations
- **Emotional regulation toolkits** should include crisis management, daily maintenance, trigger management, self-soothing, and grounding techniques for comprehensive emotional health support

Chapter 14: Relationship Recovery

The dating profile looked perfect. Professional photos, thoughtful responses to prompts, shared interests in hiking and cooking. But when Jake met Sarah for coffee, something felt off. She was charming, attentive, and seemed genuinely interested in getting to know him. Yet he found himself scanning for red flags, waiting for the other shoe to drop, convinced that her interest was either fake or would disappear once she got to know the "real" him.

This wasn't paranoia or low self-esteem talking—it was his nervous system's learned response to growing up with a borderline mother whose love came with emotional landmines. Jake had inherited relationship templates based on chaos, crisis, and conditional acceptance. Even when he met genuinely healthy people, his childhood programming told him to expect abandonment, manipulation, or explosive conflict.

Breaking free from inherited relationship patterns represents one of the most challenging aspects of recovery for adult children of personality-disordered parents. Your early experiences with love, trust, and connection become the blueprint for all future relationships—until you consciously choose to update that blueprint.

Understanding Inherited Relationship Dynamics

Research from PubMed Central and attachment studies shows that children internalize their parents' relationship patterns as normal, creating unconscious templates that guide adult relationship choices and behaviors.

These templates operate below conscious awareness, influencing:

- Who you're attracted to and why
- What behaviors feel "normal" in relationships
- How you interpret others' actions and motivations
- What you expect from love and connection

- How you handle conflict, intimacy, and boundaries

The challenging part is that these patterns often feel "right" even when they're harmful because they match your earliest learning about how relationships work.

Breaking Generational Patterns

Generational patterns in families with personality disorders often follow predictable cycles:

The Chaos Cycle Families with Cluster B disorders (Borderline, Narcissistic, Histrionic, Antisocial) often create relationship patterns based on intensity, drama, and crisis.

Children learn:

- Love involves emotional extremes and crisis management
- Calm relationships feel boring or fake
- Conflict is normal and even necessary for connection
- You must be dramatic or exceptional to earn attention and love

The Control Cycle Families with Cluster C disorders (Avoidant, Dependent, OCPD) often create relationship patterns based on rigid control, perfectionism, or emotional distance.

Children learn:

- Love requires meeting impossible standards
- Emotions are problems to be solved rather than experiences to be shared
- Autonomy threatens relationships
- Worth must be earned through performance or caretaking

The Distortion Cycle
Families with Cluster A disorders (Paranoid, Schizoid, Schizotypal) often create relationship patterns based on suspicion, isolation, or reality distortion.

Children learn:

- People can't be trusted with emotional intimacy
- Social connections are dangerous or pointless
- Normal relationship expectations are unreasonable
- Isolation is safer than vulnerability

Case Example: Breaking the Chaos Cycle

Maria, 31, grew up with a histrionic mother whose relationships were theatrical productions of passion, betrayal, reconciliation, and drama. Maria learned that love looked like soap opera storylines with constant emotional intensity.

In her twenties, Maria was consistently attracted to partners who created relationship drama—men who were unavailable, unpredictable, or emotionally volatile. Stable, kind partners felt "boring" and she would lose interest quickly, convinced that their calm affection wasn't "real love."

Maria's pattern-breaking work began with recognizing that her attraction to chaos was learned, not innate. She started paying attention to how she felt in her body around different types of people. Drama-prone partners activated her fight-or-flight system, creating an adrenaline rush she'd learned to associate with romantic excitement.

Healthy, stable partners activated her parasympathetic nervous system, creating calm connection she'd learned to interpret as boredom or disinterest.

Maria practiced staying in relationships that felt calm longer than was comfortable, giving her nervous system time to adjust to safety-based connection rather than crisis-based bonding. She learned that sustainable love felt different from dramatic love—quieter but deeper, steady rather than explosive.

The breakthrough came when Maria realized that drama-based relationships had never actually made her happy. They'd made her feel alive and important in the moment, but they'd left her exhausted, insecure, and constantly managing crisis rather than building genuine intimacy.

Identifying Inherited Dynamics

Most people aren't consciously aware of their inherited relationship patterns because they develop in early childhood before we have language or conscious memory. These dynamics feel "normal" even when they're problematic.

Common Inherited Dynamics:

Caretaking/Rescuing Patterns

- Feeling responsible for others' emotions and problems
- Being attracted to people who need "fixing" or "saving"
- Feeling worthy only when you're useful to others
- Difficulty receiving care or support from partners

People-Pleasing/Approval-Seeking Patterns

- Automatically adjusting your personality to match what others want
- Feeling anxious when someone seems disappointed or upset
- Difficulty expressing preferences that might conflict with others'
- Measuring relationship success by others' happiness rather than mutual satisfaction

Hypervigilance/Control Patterns

- Constantly monitoring partners' moods and reactions
- Trying to prevent conflict by managing others' emotions
- Feeling responsible for relationship outcomes
- Difficulty trusting others to handle their own feelings and choices

Abandonment/Engulfment Patterns

- Fearing both being left and being smothered
- Pushing people away when they get too close
- Clinging to relationships even when they're unhealthy
- Difficulty finding the middle ground between independence and connection

Case Example: Transforming the Control Cycle

David, 34, grew up with an OCPD father whose love came with performance reviews and an avoidant mother who provided practical care but no emotional warmth. David learned that relationships involved either meeting impossible standards or accepting emotional distance.

In adult relationships, David found himself either trying to be the "perfect" partner (anticipating needs, avoiding mistakes, performing rather than being authentic) or withdrawing emotionally when intimacy felt too vulnerable.

David's pattern-breaking work involved learning that he could be imperfect and still be loved. He practiced sharing his authentic thoughts and feelings even when they weren't polished or impressive. He learned to ask for what he needed rather than trying to anticipate his partner's needs.

Most importantly, David learned that emotional intimacy didn't require perfection—it required honesty, vulnerability, and the willingness to be seen as he actually was rather than as who he thought he should be.

The transformation happened when David's partner responded to his vulnerability with acceptance and affection rather than criticism or withdrawal. He realized that healthy love didn't require performance—it required presence.

Building Secure Attachments

Secure attachment in adult relationships involves the ability to be close without losing yourself and to be independent without pushing others away. It's characterized by:

- Trust that others generally have good intentions
- Comfort with emotional intimacy and physical affection
- Ability to communicate needs and boundaries directly
- Resilience during conflict—ability to repair and reconnect
- Balance between autonomy and connection

For adult children of PD parents, building secure attachment often requires conscious learning of skills that others developed naturally through healthy family modeling.

Secure Attachment Skills:

Emotional Safety Creation

- Learning to create and maintain emotional safety in relationships
- Developing the ability to self-soothe during relationship stress
- Building trust gradually through consistent, reliable behavior
- Learning to repair ruptures and reconnect after conflict

Authentic Communication

- Expressing thoughts and feelings honestly rather than strategically
- Asking for what you need directly rather than through hints or manipulation
- Listening to understand rather than to defend or fix
- Sharing vulnerability appropriately based on relationship development

Healthy Interdependence

- Maintaining individual identity within relationships
- Supporting others without losing yourself

- Accepting support without feeling burdensome
- Balancing together time and apart time

Case Example: Developing Secure Attachment

Jennifer, 29, grew up with a dependent mother who used Jennifer as her primary emotional support system and a narcissistic father who saw Jennifer as an extension of his own ego rather than a separate person.

Jennifer learned that relationships involved either being responsible for others' emotional wellbeing or performing to meet others' expectations. She'd never experienced a relationship where she could simply be herself and be accepted.

Jennifer's secure attachment development began with learning to identify and communicate her authentic feelings and needs. She practiced saying things like "I feel overwhelmed when you call me multiple times a day" instead of just feeling resentful and withdrawing.

She also learned to receive her partner's authentic expressions without taking responsibility for fixing their feelings or performing to make them feel better. When her partner felt stressed about work, Jennifer learned to offer support without trying to solve the problem or blame herself for their distress.

The breakthrough came when Jennifer realized that secure relationships could handle authenticity—both her own and her partner's. She didn't need to be perfect or constantly caretaking to maintain connection. In fact, the relationship became stronger when both people could be real rather than performative.

Conscious Parenting Approaches

Many adult children of PD parents worry about repeating harmful patterns with their own children. Conscious parenting involves making deliberate choices about how to raise children based on what you want them to learn about relationships, emotions, and self-worth.

Key Principles of Conscious Parenting:

Emotional Validation

- Acknowledging and accepting your child's emotions as valid
- Teaching emotional vocabulary and regulation skills
- Modeling healthy emotional expression and management
- Creating safety for your child to experience and express all feelings

Healthy Boundaries

- Setting limits that protect both you and your child
- Teaching children that boundaries are loving rather than rejecting
- Respecting your child's developing autonomy and individual preferences
- Modeling how to maintain relationships while honoring personal needs

Unconditional Positive Regard

- Loving your child for who they are rather than what they achieve
- Separating your child's behavior from their worth as a person
- Avoiding conditional love based on performance or compliance
- Teaching your child that they're inherently worthy of love and respect

Repair and Reconnection

- Taking responsibility when you make parenting mistakes
- Modeling how to apologize genuinely and make amends

- Teaching children that relationships can survive conflict and repair
- Demonstrating that people can change and grow rather than being fixed in patterns

Exercise: Pattern Analysis

This exercise helps you identify inherited relationship dynamics that may be affecting your current relationships.

Family of Origin Analysis: Reflect on your parents' relationship patterns:

- How did your parents handle conflict with each other?
- What did love look like in your family?
- How were emotions expressed and received?
- What happened when someone had different needs or preferences?
- How were boundaries respected or violated?

Your Current Patterns: Examine your adult relationship history:

- What type of people are you consistently attracted to?
- What relationship problems keep recurring across different partners?
- How do you handle conflict, intimacy, and independence?
- What feels "normal" in relationships even if it's not healthy?
- Which relationship behaviors do you do automatically without conscious choice?

Pattern Connections: Identify connections between family patterns and your current relationships:

- Which of your relationship behaviors mirror your parents' patterns?
- What did you swear you'd never do that you sometimes catch yourself doing?

- How do you react when relationships feel too similar to or too different from your childhood experiences?
- What relationship skills do you wish you'd learned but weren't taught?

Exercise: Communication Practice

This exercise helps you develop authentic communication skills that support secure attachment.

Authentic Expression Practice: For one week, practice expressing your authentic thoughts and feelings in low-stakes situations:

- Share a genuine preference even if it differs from others'
- Express a need directly rather than hinting or hoping others will guess
- Communicate a boundary kindly but clearly
- Share appreciation and affection without expecting specific responses

Active Listening Practice: Practice listening to understand rather than to respond:

- Ask clarifying questions to better understand others' perspectives
- Reflect back what you hear before offering your own thoughts
- Notice when you're listening to fix, defend, or advise rather than to understand
- Practice being present with others' emotions without taking responsibility for changing them

Conflict Navigation Practice: Practice addressing disagreements constructively:

- Express your perspective using "I" statements rather than "you" accusations
- Listen for the valid points in others' positions even when you disagree

- Focus on finding solutions rather than proving who's right
- Take breaks when discussions become too heated, then return to resolve issues

The Paradox of Relationship Recovery

One of the most surprising discoveries in relationship recovery is that the healthier you become, the less tolerance you have for unhealthy relationship dynamics. This can initially feel discouraging as you realize how many relationships in your life were based on dysfunctional patterns.

But this increasing discernment is actually a sign of progress. As you develop secure attachment capabilities, you naturally gravitate toward people who can meet you at that level of health and away from people who require you to return to old survival patterns.

The relationships that survive your growth become deeper and more satisfying. The relationships that end due to your healthy changes reveal that they were based on your willingness to be unhealthy rather than on genuine mutual care.

Jake, whose story opened this chapter, eventually learned to recognize the difference between his trauma responses and his genuine intuition about people. He couldn't eliminate all anxiety about new relationships, but he could choose how to respond to that anxiety.

When he met someone healthy, his nervous system's initial wariness became information to process rather than orders to follow. He could feel the anxiety and still choose to move forward with appropriate caution rather than automatic withdrawal.

Preparing for Daily Practices

Your relationship recovery work provides the foundation for the daily practices that support long-term healing. Healthy relationships both require and reinforce the emotional regulation, boundary skills, and authentic self-expression you've been developing.

The next chapter explores how to create sustainable daily practices that support your continued growth and prevent backsliding into old patterns.

Relationship Recovery Foundations

- **Inherited relationship templates** from personality-disordered families operate unconsciously, influencing attraction patterns, conflict styles, and intimacy expectations in adult relationships
- **Generational pattern breaking** requires recognizing learned dynamics like chaos cycles, control cycles, and distortion cycles that feel normal but create relationship problems
- **Secure attachment development** involves learning emotional safety creation, authentic communication, and healthy interdependence through conscious skill practice
- **Inherited dynamics identification** helps recognize automatic caretaking, people-pleasing, hypervigilance, and abandonment patterns that interfere with genuine connection
- **Conscious parenting approaches** break generational cycles through emotional validation, healthy boundaries, unconditional positive regard, and repair skills with your own children
- **Pattern analysis exercises** connect family-of-origin dynamics to current relationship challenges while communication practice builds authentic expression and active listening skills
- **Relationship recovery paradox** involves losing tolerance for unhealthy dynamics as you develop secure attachment capabilities, leading to deeper satisfaction in remaining relationships

Chapter 15: Daily Practices for Long-term Healing

The alarm went off at 6:30 AM, same as always. But instead of immediately reaching for her phone to check emails and start the day's mental to-do list, Rebecca paused. She'd been practicing this pause for three months now—a simple moment of checking in with herself before the world made its demands.

"How am I feeling this morning?" she asked herself silently. Tired, but not exhausted. A little anxious about the presentation at work. Grateful for the rain sounds against the window. It was a small practice, barely two minutes, but it was slowly changing her life.

For thirty-four years, Rebecca had lived from the outside in—constantly monitoring what others needed, what situations demanded, what problems required solving. The idea of checking in with her own internal experience felt foreign and even selfish at first. But she was learning that self-awareness wasn't selfish—it was the foundation for everything else she wanted to build.

The Science of Sustainable Change

Research from neuroscience and behavioral psychology shows that lasting change happens through consistent small practices rather than dramatic overhauls. Your brain changes through repetition—creating new neural pathways that eventually become automatic.

For adult children of personality-disordered parents, this process is particularly important because you're not just learning new skills—you're updating deeply ingrained survival patterns that developed over years or decades.

The key is creating daily practices that are:

- **Sustainable**: Small enough to maintain during stressful periods
- **Specific**: Clear actions rather than vague intentions

- **Sequential**: Building on each other to create cumulative change
- **Self-compassionate**: Designed with understanding for your specific healing needs

Creating Your Healing Routine Foundation

Your healing routine should address the four core areas that personality-disordered parenting typically disrupts: emotional awareness, self-compassion, boundary maintenance, and authentic self-expression.

Morning Practices: Setting Your Internal Foundation

Self Check-In (2-3 minutes) Begin each day by connecting with your internal experience:

- How am I feeling emotionally right now?
- What does my body need today?
- What am I looking forward to?
- What am I concerned about?
- How can I support myself today?

Intention Setting (2-3 minutes) Choose one specific way you want to practice your healing today:

- "Today I'll practice saying no to one request that would overextend me"
- "Today I'll express one authentic preference even if it differs from others'"
- "Today I'll use my coping skills if I feel triggered rather than just pushing through"
- "Today I'll celebrate one small achievement instead of immediately finding flaws"

Midday Practices: Maintaining Connection to Yourself

Emotional Temperature Check (1-2 minutes) At least once during your day, pause to assess your emotional state:

- Am I holding tension anywhere in my body?
- Have my emotions shifted since morning?
- Am I taking care of my needs or only focusing on others'?
- Do I need to adjust my approach to the rest of the day?

Boundary Moment (varies) Practice one small boundary-setting action:

- Take a five-minute break when you feel overwhelmed
- Express a preference about lunch plans or meeting times
- Say "let me think about it" instead of automatically saying yes
- End a conversation that's become draining or unproductive

Evening Practices: Integration and Self-Care

Daily Appreciation (3-5 minutes) Before bed, acknowledge your efforts and progress:

- What did I handle well today, even if imperfectly?
- How did I take care of myself or others?
- What am I grateful for about today?
- What did I learn about myself or relationships?

Preparation for Tomorrow (2-3 minutes) Set yourself up for success:

- What do I need tomorrow to feel supported?
- Is there anything I need to prepare to take care of myself?
- How can I approach tomorrow's challenges with self-compassion?

Case Example: Robert's Routine Development

Robert, 35, grew up with an avoidant mother and narcissistic father—a combination that taught him to suppress his emotional needs while performing for others' approval. As an adult, he was professionally successful but felt empty and disconnected from himself.

Robert started with a very simple morning practice: asking himself "How am I feeling?" before getting out of bed. This felt awkward at first because he'd learned that his feelings didn't matter and were probably wrong anyway.

He discovered that most mornings he felt some combination of tired, anxious, and numb—emotions he'd been pushing away for so long that he'd forgotten they existed. Instead of judging these feelings, he practiced simply acknowledging them: "I notice I'm feeling anxious about the team meeting today."

Robert added a midday practice of taking a five-minute walk outside, using this time to check in with his body and emotional state. He was surprised to discover how much tension he carried in his shoulders and jaw from constantly monitoring others' reactions to him.

His evening practice involved writing down one thing he'd done well that day and one thing he was grateful for. This was challenging because his internal critic was trained to find flaws in everything he did. But gradually, Robert began to notice and appreciate his own efforts and achievements.

The cumulative effect of these small practices was profound. Robert began to feel like he existed as a separate person with his own experiences rather than just as a performer responding to others' needs and expectations.

Support Group Navigation

Connecting with others who understand your experience can provide validation, perspective, and practical strategies that individual healing work sometimes misses.

Types of Support Groups:

Adult Children of Personality-Disordered Parents Groups These focus specifically on healing from PD family dynamics and understand the unique challenges this creates.

Adult Children of Alcoholics (ACA) Groups While focused on addiction, these groups address many similar family dysfunction patterns including emotional neglect, parentification, and boundary issues.

Codependents Anonymous (CoDA) Groups These address relationship patterns like people-pleasing, caretaking, and difficulty with boundaries that commonly develop in PD families.

Complex PTSD or Trauma Recovery Groups These focus on healing from developmental trauma and building emotional regulation skills.

What to Look For in Support Groups:

- Members who are actively working on their healing rather than just venting
- Leaders who maintain healthy boundaries and don't dominate discussions
- Focus on personal responsibility and growth rather than blaming others
- Respect for confidentiality and group guidelines
- Balance between emotional support and practical skill-building

What to Avoid:

- Groups that encourage ongoing victim mentality without growth focus
- Members who consistently dominate discussions or violate boundaries
- Leaders with poor boundaries or their own untreated mental health issues
- Groups that promote extreme approaches like permanent family cutoffs for everyone

- Settings where you feel judged or criticized rather than supported

Case Example: Maria's Support Group Journey

Maria, 31, initially resisted joining support groups because her histrionic mother had always made family problems into public drama. Maria feared that talking about her childhood would feel like repeating her mother's pattern of making everything about getting attention.

She started with an online Adult Children of Narcissists forum, which allowed her to participate anonymously and observe others' experiences before sharing her own. Reading others' stories helped Maria realize that her childhood experiences weren't normal and that her current struggles made sense given her family background.

Maria eventually joined a local Adult Children of Alcoholics group, even though her parents weren't alcoholics, because the group addressed family dysfunction patterns she recognized. She was surprised to find that many group members had similar struggles with boundaries, self-worth, and emotional regulation despite coming from different types of dysfunctional families.

The group helped Maria understand that healing was possible and gave her practical strategies for managing difficult family interactions. Most importantly, it provided her with a community of people who understood why setting boundaries with family felt so scary and difficult.

Self-Advocacy Skills Development

Self-advocacy involves speaking up for your needs, rights, and wellbeing in situations where others might not naturally consider or protect your interests.

For adult children of PD parents, self-advocacy often feels foreign or selfish because you learned to prioritize others' needs over your own. Learning to advocate for yourself is both a skill and a mindset shift.

Core Self-Advocacy Skills:

Identifying Your Needs and Rights

- Recognizing that your needs are valid and deserve consideration
- Understanding your rights in different situations (workplace, healthcare, relationships)
- Distinguishing between wants and needs to prioritize your advocacy efforts
- Learning to trust your judgment about what you need even when others disagree

Communicating Assertively

- Expressing your needs and concerns clearly and directly
- Using "I" statements to own your experience without attacking others
- Asking for what you need without excessive apology or justification
- Following through on stated consequences when boundaries are violated

Navigating Systems and Hierarchies

- Understanding how to work within organizational structures to get needs met
- Knowing when and how to escalate concerns appropriately
- Building alliances with people who can support your advocacy efforts
- Documenting important interactions to protect yourself if needed

Case Example: Jennifer's Self-Advocacy Development

Jennifer, 30, had learned from her dependent mother that asking for help was burdensome and that she should handle everything independently. When Jennifer developed chronic health issues, she struggled to advocate for appropriate medical care because she didn't want to be seen as demanding or difficult.

Jennifer's first step was recognizing that advocating for her health wasn't selfish—it was necessary. She started preparing for medical appointments by writing down her symptoms, questions, and concerns in advance rather than trying to remember everything in the moment.

She practiced using assertive language: "I need you to explain why you're recommending this treatment" instead of "Is it okay if I ask about this treatment?" She learned to repeat her concerns if they weren't addressed: "I still haven't received an answer about why my symptoms are worsening."

Most importantly, Jennifer learned that good healthcare providers want patients to advocate for themselves because it leads to better outcomes. Providers who became defensive or dismissive when she asked questions revealed their limitations rather than hers.

Community Building

Isolation is common among adult children of PD parents because dysfunctional family systems often discourage outside connections that might provide reality testing or support. Building healthy community involves gradually expanding your network of supportive relationships.

Types of Community Connections:

Professional Support Network

- Therapists, coaches, or counselors who understand trauma and family dysfunction
- Medical providers who take your concerns seriously and treat you with respect

- Professional mentors who can provide guidance and advocacy in work settings

Peer Support Network

- Friends who share similar values and treat you with consistency and respect
- Support group members who understand your healing journey
- Online communities focused on recovery and growth rather than complaining

Interest-Based Community

- People who share your hobbies, interests, or activities
- Volunteer organizations where you can contribute meaningfully
- Learning communities like classes or workshops where you can grow and connect

Spiritual or Philosophical Community

- Religious or spiritual communities that align with your beliefs and values
- Philosophy or book discussion groups that engage your intellectual interests
- Activism or cause-oriented groups where you can work toward shared goals

Exercise: Daily Check-in System

This exercise helps you create a personalized daily check-in system based on your specific healing needs.

Design Your Check-in Questions: Choose 2-3 questions for each time period that address your primary healing focus:

For Emotional Awareness:

- How am I feeling right now?
- What emotions have I noticed today?
- What is my energy level telling me?

For Self-Compassion:

- How can I be kind to myself today?
- What do I appreciate about how I've handled challenges today?
- What do I need to feel supported right now?

For Boundary Maintenance:

- Am I honoring my limits and needs?
- Where might I need to set or reinforce boundaries today?
- What am I saying yes/no to and why?

For Authentic Expression:

- Have I been honest about my thoughts and feelings today?
- What would I like to express that I've been holding back?
- How can I be more genuinely myself?

Create Your Schedule:

- Morning check-in: 2-3 minutes after waking
- Midday check-in: 1-2 minutes during lunch or afternoon break
- Evening check-in: 3-5 minutes before bed

Track Your Progress: Keep a simple log of your daily practice for one month, noting:

- Which days you completed your check-ins
- What you learned about yourself
- Changes in your emotional awareness or self-care
- Challenges that interfered with the practice

Exercise: Support Mapping

This exercise helps you identify your current support network and areas where additional support would be helpful.

Current Support Assessment: Create categories and list people in each area:

Emotional Support (people you can share feelings with):

- Who listens without trying to fix or judge?
- Who validates your experiences and feelings?
- Who provides comfort during difficult times?

Practical Support (people who help with tangible needs):

- Who can you ask for help with tasks or problems?
- Who provides resources or information when you need it?
- Who is available during emergencies?

Growth Support (people who encourage your development):

- Who celebrates your progress and achievements?
- Who challenges you to grow in healthy ways?
- Who shares similar values about personal development?

Fun and Recreation (people you enjoy spending time with):

- Who do you have fun with without drama or stress?
- Who shares your interests and hobbies?
- Who helps you relax and enjoy life?

Gap Analysis: Identify areas where your support network feels thin:

- Which categories have few or no people?
- Are you relying too heavily on one person for multiple types of support?
- What types of support would help your healing journey?

Support Building Plan: For each gap you identified, create specific actions:

- Where might you meet people who could provide this type of support?
- How can you deepen existing relationships to include more mutual support?
- What support groups or communities might address these needs?

Sustaining Your Practice

The most important aspect of daily healing practices is consistency over perfection. You don't need to do everything perfectly every day—you need to maintain connection to your healing process even during difficult periods.

Strategies for Sustainability:

Start Small Begin with practices that take less than five minutes total per day. You can always expand later, but you can't sustain what feels overwhelming from the start.

Link to Existing Habits Attach new practices to things you already do daily—check in with yourself while drinking morning coffee, practice gratitude while brushing teeth, set intentions while commuting.

Plan for Obstacles Identify likely barriers to your practice and create solutions in advance. If mornings are rushed, do your check-in the night before. If you forget, set phone reminders.

Focus on Progress, Not Perfection Missing a day doesn't ruin your progress. What matters is returning to the practice without judgment and continuing the overall pattern of self-care.

Rebecca, whose story opened this chapter, eventually expanded her simple morning check-in into a comprehensive daily practice that included mindfulness, boundary setting, emotional processing, and gratitude. But it started with that single two-minute pause before getting out of bed.

Your daily practices become the foundation for all other healing work—providing consistent support for your continued growth and preventing backsliding into old survival patterns.

Preparing for Integration

Your daily practices create the stability and self-awareness needed for the final stage of healing: integration and post-traumatic growth. The next chapter explores how to transform your painful experiences into wisdom, strength, and purpose that can benefit both you and others.

Daily Practice Foundations

- **Sustainable change** happens through consistent small practices rather than dramatic overhauls, creating new neural pathways that eventually become automatic
- **Healing routine foundation** should address emotional awareness, self-compassion, boundary maintenance, and authentic self-expression through morning, midday, and evening practices
- **Support group navigation** involves finding communities that focus on active healing rather than ongoing victim mentality, with healthy boundaries and mutual growth support
- **Self-advocacy skills** include identifying needs and rights, communicating assertively, and navigating systems to protect your interests when others might not naturally consider them
- **Community building** expands your network beyond family dysfunction through professional support, peer connections, interest-based relationships, and spiritual or philosophical communities
- **Daily check-in systems** should be personalized to your healing needs with 2-3 questions for each time period addressing your primary recovery focus areas

- **Practice sustainability** requires starting small, linking to existing habits, planning for obstacles, and focusing on progress over perfection to maintain long-term healing momentum

Chapter 16: Post-Traumatic Growth - Thriving Beyond Survival

The email notification appeared on Lisa's phone at 3:47 PM on a Tuesday. Another message from someone who had read her blog about growing up with personality-disordered parents. "Your story helped me realize I'm not crazy," the message read. "For the first time, I understand why relationships feel so hard for me. Thank you for sharing what you learned."

Lisa paused in her kitchen, holding her phone, remembering the woman she'd been five years ago—terrified of being authentic, convinced she was fundamentally broken, spending enormous energy trying to be whoever she thought others wanted her to be. That woman couldn't have imagined writing publicly about her childhood, much less helping others understand their own experiences.

This transformation represents post-traumatic growth—not just healing from wounds, but developing capabilities, wisdom, and purpose that might never have emerged without working through those difficult experiences. Lisa hadn't just recovered from her childhood trauma; she'd been changed by it in ways that allowed her to create meaning, help others, and build a life richer than she'd ever imagined possible.

Understanding Post-Traumatic Growth

Post-traumatic growth differs from resilience or recovery. Resilience involves bouncing back to your previous level of functioning. Recovery involves healing from wounds and learning to manage symptoms. Post-traumatic growth involves being changed by trauma in positive ways—developing new capacities, deeper wisdom, and expanded possibilities that wouldn't have existed without working through the difficult experiences.

Research by Richard Tedeschi and Lawrence Calhoun identifies five areas where people commonly experience growth following trauma:

1. **Appreciation of Life**: Greater gratitude for ordinary experiences and deeper engagement with daily life
2. **Relating to Others**: Enhanced empathy, deeper relationships, and increased compassion for others' struggles
3. **Personal Strength**: Recognition of your own resilience and capability to handle future challenges
4. **New Possibilities**: Discovery of interests, abilities, or life paths that were previously unconsidered
5. **Spiritual Development**: Deeper sense of meaning, purpose, or connection to something greater than yourself

For adult children of personality-disordered parents, post-traumatic growth often involves transforming survival skills into life-giving strengths and finding ways to use your hard-earned wisdom to benefit yourself and others.

From Victim to Thriver Journey

The journey from victim to thriver isn't linear or predictable. It often involves moving through several stages, sometimes cycling back through earlier phases during particularly challenging periods.

Stage 1: Survival Mode In this stage, you're primarily focused on managing symptoms, getting through daily life, and preventing further harm. Your energy goes toward basic functioning rather than growth or expansion.

Characteristics:

- Hypervigilance and constant stress management
- Difficulty seeing beyond immediate problems
- Feeling overwhelmed by basic life requirements
- Limited emotional or physical energy for growth activities

Stage 2: Recovery Focus In this stage, you're actively working on healing—attending therapy, learning new skills, understanding your family patterns, and developing healthier coping strategies.

Characteristics:

- Active engagement in therapy or self-help work
- Learning about trauma, personality disorders, and family dysfunction
- Developing emotional regulation and relationship skills
- Beginning to establish boundaries and practice self-care

Stage 3: Integration and Stabilization In this stage, new skills become more automatic, crisis episodes become less frequent and less intense, and you begin to feel like you're living your life rather than just managing it.

Characteristics:

- Consistent use of healthy coping strategies
- Stable relationships and work performance
- Reduced frequency and intensity of trauma symptoms
- Beginning to consider goals beyond basic stability

Stage 4: Growth and Expansion In this stage, you begin to discover new possibilities, interests, and purposes. Your focus shifts from healing problems to creating the life you actually want.

Characteristics:

- Exploring interests and activities you previously couldn't consider
- Taking on new challenges and responsibilities
- Developing leadership or mentorship roles
- Creating meaning from your experiences

Stage 5: Thriving and Contribution In this stage, your experiences become a source of wisdom and strength that benefits both you and others. You're not defined by your trauma, but you're informed by the growth it catalyzed.

Characteristics:

- Using your experiences to help others
- Leading by example in your relationships and community
- Creating work or projects that reflect your values and growth
- Feeling grateful for your journey, including the difficult parts

Case Example: Marcus's Transformation Journey

Marcus, 36, grew up with a paranoid father whose constant suspicion and hypervigilance taught Marcus to see threats everywhere. For years, Marcus felt cursed by his inherited anxiety and suspicious nature, which interfered with friendships, romantic relationships, and career advancement.

Marcus's journey through therapy helped him understand that his vigilant nature, while exhausting, had also developed extraordinary skills for reading people, recognizing deception, and protecting himself and others from genuine threats.

In his recovery work, Marcus learned to distinguish between inherited paranoia and appropriate caution. He didn't eliminate his observational abilities—he learned to use them consciously rather than being controlled by them.

The transformation happened when Marcus realized his childhood had given him unusual gifts for recognizing and responding to danger. He became a crisis intervention specialist, helping people navigate domestic violence situations and workplace conflicts.

Marcus's hypervigilance, which had once isolated him from others, became a professional strength that helped protect vulnerable people. His childhood experience of living with someone whose perception of reality was distorted gave him patience and understanding for clients whose judgment had been compromised by trauma or manipulation.

Marcus didn't forget his difficult childhood or minimize its impact. But he found ways to transform his survival skills into life-giving capabilities that created meaning and purpose in his adult life.

Meaning-Making from Trauma

Creating meaning from traumatic experiences involves finding ways that your difficult past can contribute to your present purpose and future goals. This doesn't require being grateful for trauma or believing that "everything happens for a reason"—it involves discovering what valuable qualities, skills, or wisdom emerged from working through your experiences.

Common Ways People Create Meaning:

Helping Others with Similar Experiences Many people find purpose in supporting others who face similar challenges—through professional work, volunteer activities, support groups, or informal mentoring.

Developing Expertise in Related Areas Some people channel their experiences into professional development in fields like psychology, social work, education, healthcare, or advocacy.

Creating Art, Writing, or Other Expression Creative expression can transform personal pain into beauty, insight, or inspiration that touches others' lives.

Advocating for System Change Some people work to change institutions, policies, or social attitudes that perpetuate the types of harm they experienced.

Modeling Healthy Relationships Breaking generational patterns and creating healthier families, friendships, or communities becomes a form of activism and contribution.

Developing Spiritual or Philosophical Understanding Some people find meaning through developing deeper understanding about human nature, suffering, growth, and purpose.

Case Example: Sarah's Meaning-Making Process

Sarah, 33, grew up with an OCPD mother whose perfectionism and criticism left Sarah feeling like she could never measure up to impossible standards. For years, Sarah's perfectionism helped her achieve professionally but also created constant anxiety and dissatisfaction.

Through recovery work, Sarah learned to recognize perfectionism as a trauma response and developed healthier relationships with achievement and failure. She learned to appreciate "good enough" and to find satisfaction in progress rather than only in flawless outcomes.

Sarah's meaning-making began when she realized how many people struggled with similar perfectionism and self-criticism. She started a blog about recovering from perfectionism, sharing practical strategies and personal insights about learning to accept imperfection.

The blog evolved into workshops for high-achieving professionals who wanted to reduce anxiety and increase satisfaction in their work. Sarah's childhood experience with impossible standards became the foundation for helping others discover that excellence didn't require perfection.

Sarah found deep satisfaction in using her hard-earned wisdom to help others avoid some of the suffering she'd experienced. Her perfectionism didn't disappear, but it became a conscious tool rather than an unconscious prison.

Helping Others Heal

Many people in post-traumatic growth phases feel called to help others who are struggling with similar challenges. This desire to help can become a meaningful part of recovery, but it requires maintaining healthy boundaries and continuing your own growth work.

Healthy Ways to Help Others:

Professional Development Pursuing training and credentials in helping professions while maintaining appropriate boundaries and self-care practices.

Peer Support Participation Sharing your experience in support groups while respecting others' autonomy and avoiding trying to "fix" people.

Creating Resources Writing, blogging, or creating other resources that people can use independently rather than creating dependent relationships.

Modeling Health Living as an example of recovery and growth rather than trying to convince others to change.

Advocacy Work Working to change systems or policies that affect people with similar experiences.

Boundaries in Helping:

Not Trying to Save Everyone Recognizing that you can't heal others and that trying to do so often recreates codependent patterns.

Maintaining Your Own Growth Continuing your own therapy, self-care, and development rather than focusing exclusively on helping others.

Respecting Others' Autonomy Offering support without trying to control others' choices or timelines for healing.

Avoiding Professional Overreach Staying within the bounds of your training and experience rather than trying to provide therapy without proper credentials.

Case Example: Jennifer's Balanced Approach to Helping

Jennifer, 32, grew up with a histrionic mother whose dramatic emotional needs taught Jennifer to be an expert emotional caretaker. In early recovery, Jennifer was drawn to helping others but quickly found herself recreating caretaking patterns.

Jennifer learned to distinguish between healthy support and codependent caretaking. Healthy support involved sharing her experience and resources while respecting others' autonomy. Caretaking involved trying to manage others' emotions and taking responsibility for their progress.

Jennifer started facilitating a support group for adult children of personality-disordered parents, but she maintained clear boundaries about her role. She shared her experience and guided discussions but didn't try to be anyone's therapist or solve their problems.

She also continued her own therapy and personal growth work, recognizing that helping others required maintaining her own emotional health and boundaries. When group members tried to make her their personal counselor, she redirected them to professional resources.

Jennifer found deep satisfaction in helping others feel less alone and more hopeful about their recovery, but she maintained the boundaries necessary to keep this work sustainable and healthy.

Setback Navigation

Post-traumatic growth doesn't mean you never have difficult days or periods of struggle. Growth often involves cycles of expansion and consolidation, with temporary setbacks that don't erase your overall progress.

Common Triggers for Temporary Setbacks:

- Major life stresses like job changes, relationship transitions, or health issues
- Family events or interactions that reactivate old patterns
- Anniversary dates of traumatic events or losses
- Situations that strongly resemble childhood trauma dynamics

Healthy Setback Navigation:

- Recognizing setbacks as temporary rather than evidence of failed progress
- Using setbacks as information about what additional support or skills you need
- Maintaining self-compassion during difficult periods rather than self-criticism
- Returning to basic self-care and coping practices rather than trying to push through
- Seeking additional support when needed without shame about needing help

Learning from Setbacks: Each difficult period can provide information about your continued growth edges and areas where additional work might be helpful. Setbacks often reveal new layers of healing work or skills that need development.

Life Vision Creation

Post-traumatic growth often involves expanding your vision of what's possible for your life beyond just managing symptoms or problems. As you stabilize in recovery, you can begin creating goals and dreams based on your authentic desires rather than just survival needs.

Components of Life Vision:

Values Clarification Identifying what matters most to you based on your authentic preferences rather than inherited expectations or survival priorities.

Relationship Vision Imagining the types of relationships you want to create and maintain, including romantic partnerships, friendships, family relationships, and community connections.

Work and Contribution Vision Considering how you want to spend your time and energy in ways that feel meaningful and aligned with your values and interests.

Personal Growth Vision Identifying areas where you want to continue developing, learning, or expanding throughout your life.

Legacy Vision Considering what you want your life to contribute to the world and how you want to be remembered.

Exercise: Values Clarification

This exercise helps you identify your authentic values separate from inherited expectations or survival priorities.

Step 1: Initial Values List From the list below, choose 10 values that feel most important to you: Adventure, Authenticity, Authority, Autonomy, Balance, Beauty, Challenge, Community, Compassion, Competence, Competition, Connection, Courage, Creativity, Curiosity, Excellence, Excitement, Faith, Fame, Family, Freedom, Friendship, Fun, Growth, Health, Honesty, Hope, Humility, Independence, Influence, Inner Harmony, Integrity, Intelligence, Intimacy, Joy, Justice, Knowledge, Leadership, Learning, Legacy, Leisure, Love, Loyalty, Money, Nature, Order, Parenting, Passion, Patience, Peace, Pleasure, Popularity, Power, Recognition, Relationships, Religion, Reputation, Respect, Responsibility, Security, Service, Spirituality, Stability, Success, Tradition, Travel, Truth, Wealth, Wisdom

Step 2: Values Refinement From your list of 10, narrow it down to your top 5 values by asking:

- Which of these values feel authentically mine versus inherited from family or society?
- Which values do I want to guide my major life decisions?
- Which values bring me energy and excitement when I think about living them?

Step 3: Values Definition For each of your top 5 values, write a personal definition of what this value means to you and how you want to express it in your life.

Step 4: Values Assessment For each value, rate how well your current life aligns with this value on a scale of 1-10. This helps identify areas where you might want to make changes to better honor your authentic priorities.

Exercise: Future Visualization

This exercise helps you imagine possibilities for your life beyond current limitations or problems.

Step 1: Ideal Day Visualization Imagine an ideal day in your life five years from now. Don't worry about being realistic—focus on what would bring you joy and satisfaction.

- Where are you living?
- How do you spend your time?
- Who are the important people in your life?
- What activities bring you energy and excitement?
- How do you feel about yourself and your life?

Step 2: Legacy Visualization Imagine you're at the end of a long, fulfilling life, looking back with satisfaction.

- What contributions are you most proud of?
- What relationships brought you the most joy?
- What experiences are you most grateful for?
- How did you use your talents and abilities?
- What would you want to be remembered for?

Step 3: Growth Edge Identification Based on your visualizations, identify areas where growth or change would help you move toward your vision:

- What skills or qualities would you need to develop?
- What fears or limitations would you need to address?
- What support or resources would be helpful?
- What small steps could you take now to move in this direction?

The Paradox of Gratitude

One of the surprising aspects of post-traumatic growth is that many people eventually feel some form of gratitude for their difficult experiences—not because they were glad to suffer, but because they value who they became through working through the challenges.

This gratitude doesn't minimize the real harm that was done or suggest that trauma is somehow "worth it." Rather, it represents an integration of your entire life story, including the parts that were painful but contributed to your strength, wisdom, and capacity for helping others.

Lisa, whose story opened this chapter, eventually felt grateful for her journey through understanding and healing her childhood experiences. She wasn't grateful for the pain her parents caused her, but she was grateful for the wisdom, empathy, and purpose that emerged from working through that pain.

Her blog became a book, which became speaking opportunities, which became a career helping others understand and heal from family dysfunction. None of this would have existed without her difficult childhood, but it also wouldn't have existed without her conscious choice to transform her pain into purpose.

The Ongoing Journey

Post-traumatic growth isn't a destination but a continued journey of expansion, contribution, and meaning-making. Your growth will continue throughout your life as you face new challenges, develop new capabilities, and find new ways to use your experiences to benefit yourself and others.

The childhood that once felt like a curse can become a source of strength, wisdom, and purpose that enriches not only your own life but the lives of others who benefit from your journey toward wholeness.

Reflection and Integration

Your journey through this book represents its own form of post-traumatic growth—taking the painful experiences of your childhood and transforming them into understanding, skills, and possibilities for creating the life you truly want.

You began this journey carrying survival patterns that once protected you but may have outlived their usefulness. Through understanding your parents' disorders, recognizing your adaptive patterns, learning therapeutic approaches, practicing reparenting, setting boundaries, regulating emotions, recovering in relationships, and creating daily practices, you've developed the foundation for thriving rather than just surviving.

The challenges you faced as a child were real and their impact was significant. But they don't define the limits of what's possible for your future. You have the opportunity to use everything you've learned—about yourself, about relationships, about healing and growth—to create a life that honors both your struggles and your strength.

Your story is still being written, and you're now the author.

- **Post-traumatic growth** involves being changed by trauma in positive ways—developing new capacities, deeper wisdom, and expanded possibilities that wouldn't have existed without working through difficult experiences
- **Victim to thriver journey** progresses through survival mode, recovery focus, integration and stabilization, growth and expansion, and thriving and contribution stages in non-linear cycles
- **Meaning-making from trauma** transforms survival skills into life-giving strengths through helping others, developing expertise, creative expression, advocacy work, modeling healthy relationships, or spiritual development
- **Helping others heal** requires healthy boundaries, continued personal growth, respecting others' autonomy, and avoiding professional overreach while offering authentic support

- **Setback navigation** involves recognizing temporary struggles as information rather than failure while maintaining self-compassion and returning to basic self-care practices
- **Life vision creation** expands possibilities beyond symptom management through values clarification, relationship goals, meaningful work, personal growth, and legacy considerations
- **Gratitude paradox** allows appreciation for growth and wisdom gained through healing work without minimizing original harm or suggesting trauma was "worth it"

Referencee

American Academy of Family Physicians. (2004). A Survey of Personality Disorders. *American Family Physician*, 70(8), 1426-1434.

American Psychiatric Association. (2024). Antisocial Personality Disorder: Often Overlooked and Untreated. *APA Clinical Blog*. Retrieved from https://www.psychiatry.org/news-room/apa-blogs/antisocial-personality-disorder-often-overlooked

Brief Lands. (2024). The Influence of Parental Perfectionism and Parenting Styles on Child Perfectionism. *International Journal of Psychiatry and Behavioral Sciences*, 18(2), Article 9318.

Cambridge University Press. (2023). Parenting and personality disorder: clinical and child protection implications. *BJPsych Advances*, 29(4), 245-256.

Cleveland Clinic Health Library. (2024). Personality Disorders: Types, Causes, Symptoms & Treatment. Cleveland Clinic Medical References.

Cleveland Clinic Health Library. (2024). Borderline Personality Disorder (BPD): Symptoms & Treatment. Cleveland Clinic Clinical Database.

Cleveland Clinic Health Library. (2024). Histrionic Personality Disorder: Causes, Symptoms & Treatment. Cleveland Clinic Mental Health Resources.

Cleveland Clinic Health Library. (2024). Antisocial Personality Disorder (ASPD): Symptoms & Treatment. Cleveland Clinic Clinical References.

Cleveland Clinic Health Library. (2024). Obsessive-Compulsive Personality Disorder (OCPD): Symptoms. Cleveland Clinic Treatment Guide.

Cleveland Clinic Health Library. (2024). EMDR Therapy: What It Is, Procedure & Effectiveness. Cleveland Clinic Treatment Resources.

EBSCO Research Starters. (2024). Schizoid personality disorder (SPD). *EBSCO Health and Medicine Collection*. Academic Database Resources.

Frontiers in Psychiatry. (2023). Parenting styles and obsessive-compulsive symptoms in college students: the mediating role of perfectionism. *Frontiers in Psychiatry*, 14, Article 1126689.

Healthline Medical Resources. (2024). Schema Therapy: Theory, Schemas, Modes, Goals, and More. *Healthline Mental Health Resources*. Clinical Practice Guide.

Journal of Developmental and Life-Course Criminology. (2016). Parents, Identities, and Trajectories of Antisocial Behavior from Adolescence to Young Adulthood. *JDLCC*, 2(3), 289-307.

Medical News Today. (2024). Family systems therapy: Definition, benefits, and more. *MDT Mental Health Resources*. Clinical Treatment Overview.

Merck Manual Professional Edition. (2024). Borderline Personality Disorder (BPD). *Merck Clinical References*. Professional Medical Database.

Merck Manual Professional Edition. (2024). Obsessive-Compulsive Personality Disorder (OCPD). *Merck Clinical Database*. Professional Treatment Guide.

National Child Traumatic Stress Network. (2023). Effects of Complex Trauma. *NCTSN Resource Collection*. Trauma Research Database.

National Institute of Mental Health. (2024). Personality Disorders Statistics. *NIMH Publication Series*. Government Research Data.

NCBI - National Center for Biotechnology Information. (2023). Borderline Personality Disorder. *StatPearls*. Treasure Island, FL: StatPearls Publishing.

NCBI - National Center for Biotechnology Information. (2023). Histrionic Personality Disorder. *StatPearls*. Treasure Island, FL: StatPearls Publishing.

NCBI - National Center for Biotechnology Information. (2023). Antisocial Personality Disorder. *StatPearls*. Treasure Island, FL: StatPearls Publishing.

NCBI - National Center for Biotechnology Information. (2023).

www.ingramcontent.com/pod-product-compliance
Lightning Source LLC
Chambersburg PA
CBHW062210080426
42734CB00010B/1861